# ALL-TIME FAVORITES

# 52

PECAN-CRUSTED CHICKEN SALAD

HAWAIIAN PORK SLIDERS WITH SPAM, PAGE 25

# CONTENTS

This book is brought to you by the editors of **CUISINE** AT HOME Magazine. To subscribe, visit **www.cuisineathome.com**

**ISBN#9798645700553**

*Cuisine at Home* **All Time Favorites** is published by Cruz Bay Publishing, Inc., 2143 Grand Ave., Des Moines, IA 50312

*Cuisine at Home* is a registered trademark of Cruz Bay Publishing, Inc.

PRINTED IN THE USA

# 76

CHOCOLATE
CAKE WITH
GLOSSY ICING

ALL-TIME **FAVORITES**

Originally from the middle of Mexico's Pacific Coast region in Jalisco, posole is a classic soup typically served at Christmas to celebrate good blessings. But why wait? This rich and hearty version is worthy of any fiesta you're planning.

## PORK POSOLE

*Make this soup a day ahead so it has a chance to develop even more flavor. Plus, if you're serving it at a party, you'll have more down time.*

Makes 8 servings (about 16 cups)
Total time: 2¹/₂–3 hours

| | |
|---|---|
| 4 | lb. bone-in pork shoulder, trimmed, cut into 1-inch chunks, and seasoned with salt and black pepper (2¹/₂ lb. trimmed) |
| 2 | Tbsp. canola oil |
| 3 | cups diced white onions |
| 3 | Tbsp. minced fresh garlic |
| 2 | tsp. *each* ground cumin and dried oregano |
| 1 | tsp. ground coriander |
| 1 | dried bay leaf |
| 4 | cups low-sodium chicken broth |
| 1 | can tomato sauce (15 oz.) |
| 1 | can diced tomatoes in juice, (14.5 oz.) |
| 1 | chipotle in adobo sauce, minced |
| 1 | Tbsp. adobo sauce |
| 2 | cans white hominy (15 oz. *each*), drained and rinsed |
| ¹/₂ | cup chopped fresh cilantro |
| 2 | Tbsp. fresh lime juice |
| | Sliced radishes and avocado |

**Brown** pork in oil in 2 batches in a large pot over medium-high heat; transfer to a plate. Reduce heat to medium, add onions, garlic, cumin, oregano, coriander, and bay leaf to pot, and sweat, covered, until onions soften, 5 minutes.

**Stir in** broth, tomato sauce, diced tomatoes, chipotle, adobo sauce, and pork; bring to a boil. Cover pot, reduce heat to low, and simmer until pork is fork-tender, 2 hours.

**Add** hominy, cilantro, and lime juice; season with salt and pepper.

**Serve** posole with radishes and avocado.

Per serving: 350 cal; 10g total fat (2g sat); 88mg chol; 966mg sodium; 29g carb (6g fiber, 9g total sugars); 34g protein

### STAFF FAVORITE

Rich and hearty, this posole is a lightly spiced soup that's full of tender pork, tomatoes, and hominy in a smoky, garlicky broth. No wonder the people on staff love it.

# OUR FAVORITE
# SOUPS &
# SANDWICHES

## LASAGNA SOUP

*This recipe blends the flavors of lasagna into a comforting bowl of soup. It's everything you'd expect in a hearty baked lasagna!*

Makes 6 servings (8 cups)
Total time: 45 minutes

| | |
|---|---|
| 1 | lb. bulk Italian sausage |
| 2 | cups chopped onions |
| 1 | cup diced carrots |
| 2 | cups sliced button mushrooms |
| 2 | Tbsp. minced fresh garlic |
| 4 | cups low-sodium chicken broth |
| 1 | can Italian-style stewed tomatoes (14.5 oz.), chopped |
| 1 | can tomato sauce (10.75 oz.) |
| 1 | cup mafalda *or* farfalle pasta |
| 2 | cups chopped fresh spinach |
| 1 | cup diced provolone cheese *or* fresh mozzarella |
| 1/4 | cup shredded Parmesan |
| 4 | tsp. thinly sliced fresh basil |

**Brown** sausage in a large pot over medium-high heat. Add onions and carrots; cook 3 minutes. Stir in mushrooms and garlic; cook 3 minutes more.

**Add** broth, stewed tomatoes, and tomato sauce; bring to a boil. Add pasta and simmer until cooked through, about 10 minutes. Stir in spinach and cook until wilted.

**To serve, place** 1/4 cup provolone into serving bowls and pour soup on top. Serve soup with Parmesan and basil.

Per serving: 380 cal; 23g total fat (9g sat); 78mg chol; 1130mg sodium; 20g carb (4g fiber, 7g total sugars); 25g protein

Amanda loves broccoli cheese soup, and with the Italian flair, she can't get enough of it.

## ITALIAN BROCCOLI-CHEESE SOUP

*You can substitute other sharp, aged cheeses that melt well, like Pecorino or Asiago, for the Parmesan.*

Makes 4 servings (about 8 cups)
Total time: 45 minutes

| | |
|---|---|
| 1 | cup diced onions |
| 1/2 | cup *each* diced celery and carrot |
| 2 | Tbsp. minced fresh garlic |
| 1 | Tbsp. dried Italian seasoning |
| 1/4 | cup olive oil |
| 1/3 | cup all-purpose flour |
| 4 | cups low-sodium chicken broth |
| 1 | bag frozen chopped broccoli (1 lb.) |
| 6 | oz. cream cheese, cubed |
| 1 | cup grated Parmesan |
| | Salt, black pepper, and fresh lemon juice to taste |

**Sweat** onions, celery, carrot, garlic, and Italian seasoning in oil in a large pot over medium-low heat until vegetables begin to soften, 5 minutes.

**Stir in** flour to coat vegetables; cook 1 minute. Gradually whisk in broth, then add broccoli. Increase heat to medium-high and bring to a simmer.

**Simmer** soup until it thickens slightly, 5–8 minutes. Reduce heat to medium. Add cream cheese, stirring until it melts. Add Parmesan; stir until it melts. Season soup with salt, pepper, and lemon juice.

Per serving: 549 cal; 38g total fat (17g sat); 73mg chol; 741mg sodium; 23g carb (4g fiber, 7g total sugars); 21g protein

So it melts faster and is easier to incorporate, cube the cream cheese before adding it to the soup.

## ROPA VIEJA STEW

Makes 6 servings (8 cups)
Total time: 1¾ hours

| | |
|---|---|
| 4 | strips thick-sliced bacon, diced |
| 1¾ | lb. flank steak, trimmed, cut into 3 pieces, and seasoned with salt and black pepper |
| 2 | cups chopped onions |
| 2 | poblano chiles, seeded and sliced |
| 1 | red bell pepper, seeded and sliced |
| 2 | Tbsp. minced fresh garlic |
| 1 | Tbsp. tomato paste |
| 1 | Tbsp. dried oregano |
| 2 | tsp. ground cumin |
| ⅓ | cup masa harina *or* all-purpose flour |
| 1 | bottle beer (12 oz.) |
| 2 | cups low-sodium beef broth |
| 1 | can black beans (15 oz.), drained and rinsed |
| ½ | cup sliced pimento-stuffed green olives |
| | Salt to taste |
| | Chopped scallions |

**Preheat** oven to 375°.

**Cook** bacon in a large ovenproof pot until crisp; transfer to a paper-towel-lined plate and set aside.

**Brown** steak in drippings, about 5 minutes per side; transfer to a plate. Add onions, chiles, and bell pepper, and cook, over medium-high heat until beginning to brown, 5 minutes. Stir in garlic, tomato paste, oregano, and cumin; cook 2 minutes, then stir in masa harina and cook 1 minute more.

**Deglaze** pot with beer, scraping up any brown bits; simmer until nearly evaporated. Stir in broth, bring to a boil, then return steak to pot; cover, transfer to oven, and braise until fork-tender, about 1 hour. Remove steak from pot, shred with 2 forks, then stir back into pot along with bacon, beans, and olives. Simmer stew on stove top until heated through, about 5 minutes; season with salt.

**Serve** stew with scallions.

Per serving: 596 calories; 22g total fat (8g sat); 142mg chol; 1106mg sodium; 36g carb (9g fiber, 6g total sugars); 58g protein

"ROPA VIEJA" [ROH-pah VY-AY-hah] means "old clothes" in Spanish, but don't let its translation fool you. With strips of chiles and peppers and polka-dotted with olives and beans, it's as warm as a well-worn flannel shirt.

Stir in your favorite beer — a lager will give it a milder flavor than a stronger beer, such as an ale.

John first tasted this classic Cuban dish in a restaurant in Miami and realized he had to recreate it for himself. Once he made it for the staff, everyone agreed that it's a winner.

## SPICY MASHED SWEET POTATOES

Makes 6 servings (about 4 cups)
Total time: 35 minutes

| | |
|---|---|
| 2 | lb. sweet potatoes, peeled, cubed |
| 3 | Tbsp. unsalted butter |
| 1 | Tbsp. brown sugar |
| 1 | jalapeño, seeded and minced |
| | Salt and black pepper to taste |

**Cook** potatoes in a saucepan of boiling salted water until fork-tender, about 15 minutes. Drain potatoes; return to pan. Cook potatoes over medium heat, stirring, to remove excess moisture, 1–2 minutes.

**Add** butter, sugar, and minced jalapeño and crush with a potato masher; season with salt and pepper.

Per serving: 284 calories; 9g total fat (5g sat); 23mg chol; 126mg sodium; 49g carb (7g fiber, 13g total sugars); 4g protein

After braising 1 hour, the flank steak should be tender enough to pull apart with forks.

Return the shredded meat to the stew base and heat through with the rest of the mixture.

## CHEESY POTATO SOUP WITH BACON & SCALLIONS

*A hint of Tabasco sauce adds a spicy kick to the cheese and potatoes.*

Makes 6 servings (9 cups)
Total time: 40 minutes

| | |
|---|---|
| 8 | oz. thick-sliced bacon, diced |
| 1 | large white onion, diced (2 cups) |
| 1 | cup minced celery |
| 1 | Tbsp. minced fresh garlic |
| 2 | Tbsp. all-purpose flour |
| 6 | cups peeled and diced russet potatoes (2 lb.) |
| 1 | Tbsp. dry mustard |
| 2 | tsp. paprika |
| 3 | cups low-sodium chicken broth |
| 1 | Tbsp. Worcestershire sauce |
| 1 | tsp. Tabasco sauce |
| 4 | cups shredded sharp Cheddar |
| 2 | cups half-and-half |
| | Salt, black pepper, and cayenne pepper to taste |
| | Minced scallions |

**Cook** bacon in a large pot until crisp. Transfer bacon to a paper-towel-lined plate. Pour off all but 2 Tbsp. drippings.

**Add** onion, celery, and garlic to pot; sweat over medium heat until onion is softened, about 5 minutes. Stir in flour; cook 1–2 minutes. Add potatoes, dry mustard, and paprika; cook, stirring to coat potatoes, 1 minute.

**Stir in** broth, Worcestershire, and Tabasco. Bring to a boil, reduce heat to medium-low, and cook, partially covered, until potatoes are fork-tender, about 15 minutes.

**Coarsely mash** potatoes, then stir in Cheddar and half-and-half until Cheddar is melted, 2 minutes. Remove soup from heat; season with salt, black pepper, and cayenne. Serve soup with bacon and scallions.

Per serving: 705 cal; 44g total fat (26g sat); 137mg chol; 1231mg sodium; 36g carb; (6g fiber, 6g total sugars); 40g protein

## GOOD TO KNOW

Searing the beef in batches over high heat helps the pieces caramelize quickly and stay juicy on the inside.

## OLD-FASHIONED VEGETABLE BEEF SOUP

*Hearty and dependable, this robust classic is a satisfying blend of tender beef, hearty potatoes, and versatile vegetables.*

Makes 6 servings (12 cups)
Total time: 45 minutes

### SEAR:

- 1 lb. flat iron *or* rib-eye steak, cubed, and seasoned with salt and black pepper
- 2 Tbsp. olive oil
- 2 cups diced onions
- 1 Tbsp. minced fresh garlic
- 3 cups chopped green cabbage
- 1 yellow bell pepper, diced
- 1 cup sliced celery
- 1 cup sliced carrots
- 1 tsp. *each* dried basil, oregano, and thyme

### STIR IN:

- 4 cups low-sodium beef broth
- 2 cups peeled and diced russet potatoes
- 1 can diced tomatoes in juice (14.5 oz.)
- 1 Tbsp. Worcestershire sauce

### MASH:

- 3 Tbsp. all-purpose flour
- 2 Tbsp. unsalted butter, softened
- 1 Tbsp. tomato paste
- 4 oz. green beans, trimmed, halved, and blanched
  Salt and black pepper to taste
  Chopped fresh parsley

**Sear** beef on all sides in a large pot over medium-high heat in two batches, using 1 Tbsp. oil per batch. Transfer beef to a plate.

**Add** onions and garlic to pot; sweat over medium heat until softened, 5 minutes. Stir in cabbage, bell pepper, celery, carrots, basil, oregano, and thyme; sweat, partially covered, 10 minutes.

**Stir in** broth, potatoes, tomatoes, and Worcestershire. Bring soup to a boil, reduce heat, and simmer, partially covered, until potatoes are fork-tender, 15 minutes. Stir in beef.

**Mash** together flour, butter, and tomato paste. Bring soup to a boil, add flour mixture, and cook until thickened, 2 minutes; stir in beans. Season soup with salt and pepper and serve with parsley.

Per serving: 336 cal; 15g total fat (5g sat); 62mg chol; 344mg sodium; 30g carb; (5g fiber, 9g total sugars); 23g protein

Teresa loves both the Indian-spiced chicken noodle and the Cincinnati Chili. They share a few things in common — warm spices, pasta, and take less than an hour to prepare.

## GOOD TO KNOW

Sweating the curry powder with the vegetables helps distribute and release its flavor into the soup.

## CURRY CHICKEN NOODLE SOUP

*If you're sensitive to heat, limit the jalapeño to just half of one or leave it out entirely. If, however, you want more heat, leave the seeds in the jalapeño.*

Makes 8 servings (about 12 cups)
Total time: about 30 minutes

| | |
|---|---|
| 1 | cup *each* diced onions and red bell peppers |
| 3 | Tbsp. curry powder |
| 3 | Tbsp. minced fresh ginger |
| 3 | Tbsp. seeded and minced jalapeño (about 1 jalapeño) |
| 2 | Tbsp. minced fresh garlic |
| 2 | Tbsp. olive oil |
| 8 | cups low-sodium chicken broth |
| 8 | oz. frozen or dry kluski *or* egg noodles |
| 2 | cups shredded rotisserie chicken |
| 2 | cups chopped fresh spinach |
| 1/4 | cup chopped fresh cilantro |
| | Fresh lime juice, salt, and black pepper to taste |

**Sweat** onions, bell peppers, curry powder, ginger, jalapeño, and garlic in oil in a large pot over medium-low heat until onions begin to soften, about 3 minutes.

**Stir in** broth, cover pot, increase heat to high, and bring soup to a boil. Add noodles and cook according to package directions, about 10 minutes.

**Add** chicken, spinach, and cilantro; stir just to heat through. Season soup with lime juice, salt, and black pepper.

Per serving: 239 cal; 6g total fat (1g sat); 34mg chol; 167mg sodium; 26g carb (3g fiber, 4g total sugars); 18g protein

## CINCINNATI CHILI

*Loaded with "sweet" spices like cinnamon, allspice, and cloves, this chili isn't your typical bowl of red — it's so much better and still brings a little heat!*

Makes 4 servings (5 cups)
Total time: 45 minutes

| | |
|---|---|
| 2 | small yellow onions, chopped |
| 5 | cloves garlic |
| 1 1/2 | lb. ground round |
| 2 | Tbsp. *each* unsweetened cocoa powder, Worcestershire sauce, and cider vinegar |
| 1 | Tbsp. *each* chili powder, tomato paste, and sugar |
| 2 | tsp. ground cumin |
| 1 | tsp. *each* ground cinnamon and celery salt |
| 1/2 | tsp. *each* ground allspice and cayenne pepper |
| 1/4 | tsp. ground cloves |
| 2 | cups water |
| 1 | can tomato sauce (15 oz.) |
| | Cooked spaghetti |
| | Shredded Cheddar |
| | Diced red onions |

**Pulse** yellow onions and garlic in a food processor until minced. Add round; process until paste-like. Transfer beef mixture to a skillet and cook over medium-low heat until no longer pink; drain drippings and return to skillet.

**Add** cocoa, Worcestershire, vinegar, chili powder, tomato paste, sugar, cumin, cinnamon, celery salt, allspice, cayenne, and cloves; cook 5 minutes. Stir in water and tomato sauce; bring chili to a simmer over medium heat and cook until slightly thickened, about 25 minutes.

**Serve** chili on spaghetti topped with Cheddar and red onions.

Per serving: 1188 cal; 47g total fat (23g sat); 191mg chol; 1547mg sodium; 115g carb (4g fiber, 20g total sugars); 79g protein

# CHEERS FOR
# CHEESE
# BURGERS

We found a definite flavor theme to some of our favorite selections. The CHEESEBURGER, in all its forms, was suggested more than a few times. From soup to meatloaf, and burgers to egg rolls, you'll find plenty of ways to satisfy your craving for America's quintessential comfort food.

## CHEESEBURGER SOUP

*When it comes to cheese soups, boiling is an enemy because it can cause curdling. Once the cheese is added, just let the soup gently simmer.*

Makes 6 servings (8$\frac{1}{2}$ cups)
Total time: 35 minutes

**MELT:**
1    Tbsp. unsalted butter
1    lb. ground sirloin
1    cup diced onions
3/4  cup diced celery
1/2  cup diced carrot
1    tsp. minced fresh garlic

**STIR IN:**
3    cups low-sodium chicken broth
2    cups peeled and diced russet potatoes
1    tsp. dried basil

**MELT:**
3    Tbsp. unsalted butter
1/4  cup all-purpose flour
1$\frac{1}{2}$  cups whole milk

**ADD:**
2    cups grated Cheddar
1/4  cup ketchup
2    Tbsp. yellow mustard
      Salt and black pepper to taste
      Chopped dill pickles
      Shoestring Fries

**Melt** 1 Tbsp. butter in a large pot over medium heat. Add sirloin and cook until brown. Add onions, celery, carrot, and garlic; sweat over medium-low heat, partially covered, 10 minutes.

**Stir in** broth, potatoes, and basil; bring to a boil, reduce heat to medium, and cook until potatoes are fork-tender, 10–12 minutes.

**Melt** 3 Tbsp. butter in a saucepan over medium heat. Whisk in flour; cook 1–2 minutes. Whisk in milk until smooth. Add milk mixture to soup; cook until thickened, 3–4 minutes. Reduce heat to medium-low.

**Stir in** Cheddar, ketchup, and mustard until cheese melts; season soup with salt. Top soup with pickles and fries.

Per serving: 438 calories; 25g total fat (14g sat); 103mg chol; 498mg sodium; 25g carb (2g fiber, 8g total sugars); 28g protein

**ONLINE EXTRA**
Get the Shoestring Fries recipe and more at **CuisineAtHome.com**.

Use a wooden spoon to break up the large chunks while browning the meat to avoid clumping.

To ensure a smooth soup without lumps, make the roux in a separate pot then stir into soup.

To enhance the soup with more cheeseburger flavor, stir ketchup and mustard in at the end.

**STAFF FAVORITE**

Who would have imagined that a classic blue plate special could morph so successfully into a bowl of soup? Cheeseburger Soup started out as a playful idea, but ended up a staff hit.

WE LOVE
# MEATLOAF

Whether you're a lover of meatloaf, or not, you're going to fall head-over-heels for this one. Inspired by the FLAVORS OF A CHEESEBURGER, it's stuffed with Cheddar, bacon, pickles, and onions, then topped with a sweet, ketchup-mustard glaze. What's not to love?!

## CHEESEBURGER MEATLOAF

*This meatloaf is the perfect ratio of tender, yet firm, and it's so easy to prepare. But the best part about it is that it makes a great "day after" sandwich.*

Makes 6 servings
Total time: 1¹/₂ hours

**FOR THE MEATLOAF, COMBINE:**

| | |
|---|---|
| 1¹/₂ | lb. ground chuck |
| 10 | strips bacon, cooked and crumbled |
| 8 | oz. Cheddar, diced |
| ³/₄ | cup quick-cooking oats |
| ¹/₂ | cup *each* chopped onion and dill pickles |
| ¹/₂ | cup dill pickle juice |
| ¹/₄ | cup mayonnaise |
| 2 | eggs, lightly beaten |
| 1 | Tbsp. Worcestershire sauce |
| 1 | tsp. black pepper |
| ¹/₂ | tsp. red pepper flakes |

**FOR THE GLAZE, STIR:**

| | |
|---|---|
| ¹/₂ | cup ketchup |
| ¹/₄ | cup yellow mustard |
| 2 | Tbsp. light brown sugar |
| | Chopped pickles, *optional* |

**Preheat** oven to 375°. Line a baking sheet with foil. Lightly coat an 8¹/₂×4¹/₂-inch loaf pan with nonstick spray. Line pan with plastic wrap, allowing excess to hang over edges.

**For the meatloaf, combine** chuck, bacon, Cheddar, oats, onion, pickles, pickle juice, mayonnaise, eggs, Worcestershire, black pepper, and pepper flakes in a bowl.

**Press** meatloaf mixture into prepared pan, then carefully invert onto prepared baking sheet and discard plastic wrap. Gently reshape meatloaf as necessary.

**For the glaze, stir** together ketchup, mustard, and brown sugar; spread over meatloaf.

**Bake** meatloaf until a thermometer inserted into the center registers 160°, about 1 hour. Let meatloaf rest 10 minutes before topping with chopped pickles and slicing.

Per serving: 761 cal; 57g total fat (22g sat); 209mg chol; 1175mg sodium; 19g carb (2g fiber, 11g total sugars); 37g protein

Pat the meat mixture into the pan, being sure to press it into the corners for the sturdiest loaf.

Spread the topping over the exterior of the meatloaf to keep it moist and add more cheeseburger flavor.

## BUTTERMILK MASHED POTATOES WITH DILL & LEMON

Makes 6 servings
Total time: 20 minutes

| | |
|---|---|
| 2 | lb. Yukon gold potatoes, peeled and cubed |
| ¹/₂ | cup buttermilk, warmed |
| ¹/₂ | cup sour cream |
| 1 | Tbsp. chopped fresh dill |
| ¹/₂ | tsp. minced lemon zest |
| | Salt and black pepper to taste |

**Cook** potatoes in a pot of boiling salted water until fork-tender, 10–15 minutes. Drain potatoes and return to pot over medium-low heat, stirring to remove excess moisture, 1–2 minutes.

**Stir** buttermilk, sour cream, dill, and zest into potatoes, then mash to desired consistency; season with salt and pepper.

Per serving: 176 cal; 4g total fat (3g sat); 15mg chol; 37mg sodium; 28g carb (2g fiber, 2g total sugars); 5g protein

Want to make plain cheeseburgers extra special? Give the meat a bold kick of flavor by mixing in pimentos. And instead of laying cheese on top of the burgers, turn them "outside in" by STUFFING CHEDDAR INSIDE!

## CHEDDAR-STUFFED PIMENTO BURGERS WITH SCALLION MAYONNAISE

Makes 4 servings
Total time: 2½–3 hours

**FOR THE MAYONNAISE, STIR:**
½   cup mayonnaise
½   cup sliced scallion greens
1    tsp. Tabasco sauce
½   tsp. sugar

**FOR THE BURGERS, MIX:**
1¼  lb. ground chuck
2    jars sliced pimentos
     (4 oz. *each*), drained
     Salt and black pepper

**TOP:**
8    slices white Cheddar (4 oz.)
4    tsp. unsalted butter

**TOAST:**
4    Kaiser rolls, split
     Green leaf lettuce
     Tomato slices

**For the mayonnaise, stir** together mayonnaise, scallions, Tabasco, and sugar; chill.

**For the burgers, mix** together chuck and pimentos in a bowl; season with salt and pepper. Shape meat into 8 patties, sized to fit rolls.

**Top** 4 patties with Cheddar, then top with remaining patties; seal burgers well with a fork.

**Preheat** a cast-iron skillet over medium-high. Add burgers to skillet; cook 6 minutes. Flip burgers, top each with 1 tsp. butter, and cook 6 minutes more. Transfer burgers to a platter.

**Toast** rolls in skillet, cut sides down, until golden. Serve burgers on toasted rolls with Scallion Mayonnaise, lettuce, and tomatoes.

Per serving: 677 cal; 42g total fat (13g sat); 121mg chol; 769mg sodium; 34g carb; (3g fiber, 3g total sugars); 40g protein

**TOPPING BURGERS WITH BUTTER** AS THEY FINISH COOKING IS A MIDWESTERN TRADITION THAT'S DEFINITELY WORTH A TRY.

## CHEESEBURGER EGG ROLLS

*These egg rolls can be frozen after forming, but thaw completely before frying to ensure they cook through.*

Makes about 15 egg rolls
Total time: 1 hour + frying

**HEAT:**
    Canola oil
**BROWN:**
1    lb. ground sirloin
1    Tbsp. olive oil
**OFF HEAT, STIR IN:**
1    bag shredded iceberg
    lettuce (8 oz.)
$^1/_2$    cup diced dill pickles
$^1/_2$    cup diced onion
    Salt and black pepper to taste
**WHISK:**
1    egg
2    Tbsp. water
**ASSEMBLE:**
15    slices American cheese
15    egg roll wraps
    Sesame seeds

**Heat** canola oil in a large pot over medium-high to 375°.

**Brown** sirloin in olive oil in a sauté pan over high heat, 5 minutes.

**Off heat, stir in** lettuce, pickles, and onion; season with salt and pepper. Stir mixture until lettuce wilts; drain through a sieve and set aside to cool.

**Whisk** together egg and water for the egg wash.

**Assemble** egg rolls by placing a cheese slice in center of each egg roll wrap; top with $^1/_4$ cup sirloin mixture. Roll egg rolls according to package directions. Brush edges with egg wash to seal.

**Brush** tops of egg rolls with egg wash; sprinkle with sesame seeds.

**Fry** egg rolls in batches of 3 or 4 until golden brown, $1^1/_2$ minutes. Serve egg rolls with Special Sauce.

Per egg roll: 187 cal; 15g total fat (4g sat); 42mg chol; 332mg sodium; 5g carb; (0g fiber, 1g total sugars); 10g protein

## SPECIAL SAUCE

Makes $1^1/_2$ cups
Total time: 10 minutes

1    cup mayonnaise
$^1/_4$    cup ketchup
3    Tbsp. yellow mustard
2    Tbsp. minced shallots
$^1/_4$    cup finely diced dill pickles
    Salt and black pepper to taste

**Whisk** together mayonnaise, ketchup, mustard, shallots, and pickles. Season sauce with salt and pepper.

Per Tbsp.: 64 cal; 7g total fat (1g sat); 3mg chol; 127mg sodium; 1g carb; (0g fiber, 1g total sugars); 0g protein

**19**

STAFF FAVORITE

This is Maddy's go-to recipe for a quick, yet satisfying meal, that her whole family loves.

## CHICKEN & BACON BURRITOS WITH CHIPOTLE DRESSING

*This adaptation of a BLT ups the flavor by including chicken, cucumbers, and a chipotle ranch dressing.*

Makes 4 servings (4 burritos)
Total time: 25 minutes

| | |
|---|---|
| 4 | strips thick-sliced bacon, diced |
| 1 | lb. boneless, skinless chicken breasts, sliced into strips, seasoned with salt and black pepper |
| 3 | cups shredded romaine lettuce |
| 1/2 | cup halved grape tomatoes |
| 1/2 | cup seeded, sliced cucumber |
| 1/3 | cup purchased ranch dressing |
| 2 | tsp. diced chipotle in adobo sauce |
| 4 | burrito-sized flour tortillas (10-inch) |

**Cook** bacon in a sauté pan until crisp; transfer to a paper-towel-lined plate and drain all but 2 Tbsp. drippings.

**Sauté** chicken in drippings in same pan over medium-high heat until browned and cooked through, 8 minutes. Transfer chicken to a plate, tent with foil, and let rest 3 minutes.

**Combine** romaine, tomatoes, cucumber, and bacon in a bowl. Mix together ranch dressing and chipotle; toss with salad mixture and chill until ready to serve.

**Heat** tortillas in a large nonstick skillet, 1 minute per side.

**Divide** chicken among tortillas, top with salad mixture, and roll tortilla over filling. Halve burritos to serve.

Per serving: 485 cal; 19g total fat (5g sat); 103mg chol; 1074mg sodium; 40g carb (1g fiber, 4g total sugars); 38g protein

# MINI STEAK SANDWICHES WITH HORSERADISH SAUCE

*With an apple marinade and a mild but addictively delicious sauce, these baby sandwiches pack so much flavor, any ploughman would love them.*

Makes 12 sandwiches
Total time: 30 minutes + marinating

**FOR THE MARINADE, WHISK:**

| | |
|---|---|
| 1 | cup apple juice |
| 1/4 | cup *each* cider vinegar and olive oil |
| 3 | Tbsp. minced fresh garlic |
| 2 | Tbsp. *each* Worcestershire sauce, Dijon mustard, and honey |
| 1 | Tbsp. *each* minced fresh rosemary and kosher salt |
| 1 | tsp. black pepper |

**ADD:**

| | |
|---|---|
| 1 1/2 | lb. flank steak, trimmed and lightly scored |

**FOR THE SAUCE, WHISK:**

| | |
|---|---|
| 1/2 | cup sour cream |
| 2 | Tbsp. *each* mayonnaise and prepared horseradish |
| 1 | Tbsp. Dijon mustard |

**FOR THE SANDWICHES, ARRANGE:**

| | |
|---|---|
| 12 | cocktail buns, split |
| | Green leaf lettuce, sliced Cheddar, and thinly sliced Pink Lady apple |

STAFF FAVORITE — Pam loves a Ploughman — rare beef, Cheddar cheese, and horseradish sauce, pure yum.

**For the marinade, whisk** together apple juice, vinegar, oil, garlic, Worcestershire, Dijon, honey, rosemary, salt, and pepper; pour into a 9×13-inch baking dish.

**Add** steak to marinade; toss to coat and cover with plastic wrap. Marinate steak in the refrigerator 8 hours, or overnight, flipping occasionally. Remove dish from refrigerator 30 minutes prior to grilling, then remove steak from the marinade.

**Preheat** grill to high. Brush grill grate with oil.

**For the sauce, whisk** together sour cream, mayonnaise, horseradish; season with salt and pepper.

**Season** steak with salt and pepper, then grill, covered, until medium-rare, 4–6 minutes per side.

**Transfer** steak to a cutting board; tent with foil and let rest 5 minutes. Thinly slice steak against the grain.

**For the sandwiches, arrange** lettuce leaves on bottom buns; top with steak, Cheddar, apples, a dollop of sauce, and top buns.

Per sandwich: 329 cal; 16g total fat (5g sat); 52mg chol; 838mg sodium; 29g carb (2g fiber, 10g total sugars); 19g protein

Scoring the flank steak's smooth surface with shallow cuts allows the marinade to penetrate better.

## CROQUE MONSIEUR WITH DIJON BÉCHAMEL

*Ooo-la-la! The French really know what they're doing when it comes to ham and cheese sandwiches.*

Makes 4 servings
Total time: 40 minutes

**FOR THE BÉCHAMEL, MELT:**

4    Tbsp. unsalted butter
1/4   cup all-purpose flour

**WHISK:**

2    cups milk
2    Tbsp. Dijon mustard
1/4   tsp. freshly grated nutmeg
     Salt and black pepper to taste

**FOR THE SANDWICHES, SPREAD:**

4    Tbsp. unsalted butter, softened
8    slices artisan-style white bread
8    slices cooked ham (12 oz.)
4    oz. shredded Gruyère (about 2 cups)
     Chopped fresh parsley

**Preheat** broiler to high with rack 6 inches from element. Line a baking sheet with foil.

**For the béchamel, melt** butter in a saucepan over medium heat until foamy; whisk in flour and cook roux 1 minute.

**Whisk** milk into pan in a steady stream until completely combined, then whisk in Dijon and nutmeg. Season béchamel with salt and pepper and cook until slightly thickened, 2–3 minutes.

**For the sandwiches, spread** both sides of bread slices with butter and season with pepper. Broil bread on prepared baking sheet until golden on both sides, 2–3 minutes per side.

**Cover** one side of bread slices with 2 Tbsp. béchamel; top each with 1 slice ham, 2 Tbsp. Gruyère, and remaining béchamel. Broil sandwiches until cheese is brown and bubbly, 5–7 minutes.

**Stack** one open-faced sandwich on top of another to form one double-decker sandwich; repeat with remaining open-faced sandwiches. Top sandwiches with parsley.

Per serving: 771 cal; 43g total fat (23g sat); 156mg chol; 1409mg sodium; 53g carb (6g fiber, 13g total sugars); 40g protein

## GRILLED BROCCOLI & RED ONION HOAGIES

*There are many beliefs about where the name "hoagie" came from. One theory is that it was a sandwich so big that "you had to be a hog to eat it."*

Makes 4 servings
Total time: 30 minutes

**GRILL:**

3 cups broccoli florets, tossed with olive oil
1 medium red onion, cut into ¹/₂-inch-thick slices, and brushed with olive oil
  Salt and black pepper to taste

**BRUSH:**

4 whole-wheat hoagie rolls, split
¹/₄ cup *each* mayonnaise and Dijon mustard
2 cups shredded sharp Cheddar
¹/₂ cup sliced banana pepper rings

**Preheat** grill to medium-high. Brush grill grate with oil.
**Grill** broccoli and onion, covered, until slightly charred, 3 minutes per side; transfer to a bowl and season with salt and pepper.
**Brush** rolls with mayonnaise and Dijon, sprinkle on Cheddar, then grill, cheese sides up, until cheese melts, 1–2 minutes.
**Divide** broccoli, onion, and pepper rings among rolls and serve.

Per serving: 622 cal; 36g total fat (15g sat); 55mg chol; 1285mg sodium; 56g carb (11g fiber, 10g total sugars); 22g protein

"Who knew a sandwich featuring broccoli could be so good? But this creation reached new culinary heights in the Test Kitchen, and even with me, the most ardent meat eater."

Chris Hennessey
Senior Photographer

## ITALIAN JOE ON CIABATTA BREAD

*Full of sweet sausage and herbs, this Italian version of the classic Sloppy Joe only gets better with time, so it's ideal for making ahead. Just reheat it when ready to serve.*

Makes 12 servings (10 cups)
Total time: 1¼ hours

| | |
|---|---|
| 1¼ | lb. sweet link Italian sausage, casings removed |
| 1 | lb. ground chuck |
| 4 | Tbsp. olive oil, divided |
| 2 | cups diced onions |
| 2 | Tbsp. minced fresh garlic |
| 1 | cup diced red bell peppers |
| ½ | cup *each* diced carrot and celery |
| 2 | Tbsp. tomato paste |
| 1 | can tomato purée (28 oz.) |
| 1 | can diced tomatoes in juice (28 oz.) |
| 4 | tsp. dried oregano |
| 2 | tsp. red pepper flakes |
| 1 | tsp. *each* ground nutmeg and dried Italian seasoning |
| ½ | cup dry red wine |
| 3 | Tbsp. balsamic vinegar |
| 2 | Tbsp. brown sugar |
| | Salt and black pepper to taste |
| 2 | loaves ciabatta bread (*each* 16-inch) |

**Brown** sausage and chuck in 2 Tbsp. oil in a large pot over medium-high heat, breaking up any large chunks with a spoon, 10–15 minutes. Transfer meat to a paper-towel-lined plate. Discard drippings.

**Heat** remaining 2 Tbsp. oil in same pot over medium-high. Sauté onions until just beginning to brown, 5–10 minutes. Add garlic; cook 1 minute. Stir in bell peppers, carrot, celery, and tomato paste; cook until vegetables are softened, about 10 minutes.

**Stir in** tomato purée, diced tomatoes, oregano, pepper flakes, nutmeg, Italian seasoning, and browned meat; simmer 10 minutes.

**Add** wine, vinegar, and brown sugar, then bring mixture to a boil. Simmer sauce until thickened, 10–15 minutes, stirring often; season with salt and black pepper.

**Slice** ciabatta loaves lengthwise. Spoon Italian Joe over bottom halves of bread, cover with top halves, and cut each loaf into 6 sandwiches.

Per serving: 437 cal; 12g total fat (4g sat); 38mg chol; 840mg sodium; 58g carb (5g fiber, 11g total sugars); 25g protein

**STAFF FAVORITE** — Whether for tailgating or entertaining, this is Haley's choice to serve at any gathering.

Slice the sausage lengthwise to pierce the casing, then simply pull the casing off with your fingers.

## HAWAIIAN PORK SLIDERS WITH SPAM

*With the flavors of ham and roast pork, Spam makes this sandwich extra special.*

Makes 12 sliders
Total time: 30 minutes

| | |
|---|---|
| 1½ | lb. ground pork |
| 2 | Tbsp. minced fresh ginger |
| 4 | scallions |
| | Salt and black pepper |
| 2 | Tbsp. olive oil |
| 3 | slices Swiss cheese, quartered |
| 12 | slices Spam (2x2-inch *each*) |
| | Purchased barbecue sauce |
| 12 | split and toasted King's Hawaiian sweet rolls |
| | Leaf lettuce |

**Mince** pork, ginger, and scallions in a food processor; shape into a 4x12-inch rectangle, then cut into 12 patties, and season with salt and black pepper.

**Heat** 1 Tbsp. oil in a cast-iron skillet over medium-high. Fry half the patties until cooked through, 3–4 minutes per side; repeat with remaining 1 Tbsp. oil and patties.

**Transfer** sliders to a platter, top each with a quartered Swiss cheese slice, and cover with foil to keep warm. Sear Spam in same skillet over medium heat, 1 minute per side. Spread barbecue sauce onto cut sides of rolls; layer each with lettuce, pork patty, Spam, and pico.

Per slider: 331 cal; 22g total fat (9g sat); 71mg chol; 323mg sodium; 50g carb (0g fiber, 1g total sugars); 16g protein

# HAWAIIAN PICO DE GALLO

Combine ½ cup diced pineapple, ¼ cup diced red bell pepper, and 2 Tbsp. sliced scallion greens.

STAFF
FAVORITE

Teresa is a lover of French Dips. When she can't get Cole's version from Los Angeles, she makes this one.

# FRENCH DIP AU JUS

*If you have the time, cook a one-pound beef eye of round roast in the oven at 400 degrees until medium-rare, 20–25 minutes.*

Makes 4 servings
Total time: 25 minutes

**FOR THE JUS, SAUTÉ:**

| | |
|---|---|
| 1/2 | cup *each* diced onion, celery, and carrot |
| 1 | Tbsp. olive oil |
| 1 | Tbsp. minced fresh garlic |
| 2 | tsp. tomato paste |
| 2 | cups low-sodium beef broth |
| 1 | dried bay leaf |
| 1 | tsp. Worcestershire sauce |
| 1 | tsp. beef base (such as Better Than Bouillon) |
| | Salt and black pepper to taste |

**FOR THE SANDWICHES, BRUSH:**

| | |
|---|---|
| 4 | hoagie rolls, split |
| 3–4 | Tbsp. unsalted butter, melted Coarse salt |
| 1 | lb. thinly sliced cooked roast beef |
| 4 | slices Swiss cheese |

**Preheat** broiler to high with rack 6 inches from element. Line a baking sheet with foil.

**For the jus, sauté** onion, celery, and carrot in oil in a saucepan over medium-high heat until softened, 3–4 minutes. Stir in garlic and tomato paste; cook 1 minute. Add broth, bay leaf, Worcestershire, and beef base to pan; bring to a boil. Reduce heat; simmer jus until reduced by half, 10 minutes. Strain jus and return to pan; season with salt and pepper and keep warm.

**For the sandwiches, brush** rolls, inside and outside, with melted butter and sprinkle tops with coarse salt. Broil rolls on prepared baking sheet until toasted, about 1 minute per side. Divide beef among bottom rolls and top with cheese; broil until cheese is bubbly, 2–3 minutes, then add top rolls. Slice French Dips in half and serve with jus.

Per serving: 528 cal; 26g total fat (11g sat); 81mg chol; 1284mg sodium; 28g carb; (3g fiber, 8g total sugars); 32g protein

## CELERY SLAW

*So the celery stays crisp, prepare the slaw right before serving it.*

Makes 4 servings (5 cups)
Total time: 10 minutes

| | |
|---|---|
| 1/2 | cup canola oil mayonnaise |
| 2 | Tbsp. cider vinegar |
| 1 | Tbsp. sugar |
| 1/2 | tsp. Dijon mustard |
| | Salt and black pepper to taste |
| 4 | cups coleslaw mix |
| 1 | cup sliced celery |
| 1/4 | cup sliced fresh chives |

**Whisk** together mayonnaise, vinegar, sugar, and Dijon; season with salt and pepper.

**Add** coleslaw mix, celery, and chives; toss to combine.

Per serving: 110 cal; 8g total fat (0g sat); 0mg chol; 272mg sodium; 7g carb; (2g fiber, 5g total sugars); 1g protein

Adding tomato paste and cooking it with the mirepoix gives the jus body and deep, rich flavor.

To add extra flavor, brush both sides of rolls with melted butter, sprinkle with salt, then broil to toast.

27

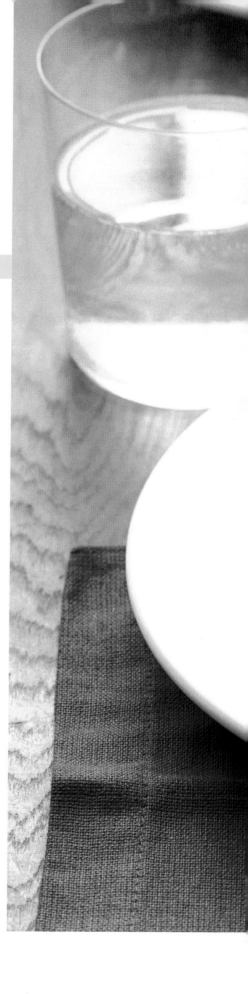

If you like chicken cutlets, pasta, tomatoes, and a quick recipe, this classic Italian dish will fit perfectly into your dinner routine. Enhanced with vodka, broth, cream, and lemon juice, this sauce is over-the-top delicious.

## CHICKEN POMODORO

*If you don't like to cook with alcohol or don't have it on hand, you can replace the vodka with more chicken broth.*

Makes 4 servings
Total time: 30 minutes

**SEASON:**
2    boneless, skinless chicken breasts, halved, pounded to 1/4-inch thick (8 oz. *each*)
    Salt and black pepper
2    Tbsp. all-purpose flour

**HEAT:**
2    Tbsp. olive oil

**OFF HEAT, DEGLAZE:**
1/4    cup vodka

**ADD:**
1/2    cup low-sodium chicken broth
1/4    cup heavy cream
1    cup halved cherry tomatoes
2    Tbsp. fresh lemon juice
1/4    cup minced scallions

**Season** cutlets with salt and pepper, then dust with flour.

**Heat** oil in a sauté pan over medium-high. Add cutlets and brown, 2–3 minutes per side; transfer to a plate.

**Off heat, deglaze** pan with vodka, scraping up any brown bits. Return pan to burner and cook vodka until nearly evaporated.

**Add** broth and cream and reduce until thickened, 2–3 minutes. Stir in tomatoes and lemon juice and bring to a simmer. Return cutlets to pan and heat until warmed through, 1 minute per side.

**Serve** cutlets with sauce and top with scallions.

Per serving: 307 cal; 15g total fat (5g sat); 100mg chol; 67mg sodium; 6g carb (1g fiber, 2g total sugars); 27g protein

### READER FAVORITE

We receive requests from our readers for this recipe on a regular basis. And we understand why.

# OUR FAVORITE
# MAIN DISH
# MEALS

# KOREAN BULGOGI TACOS

*Made popular on the streets of Los Angeles, these explosive-tasting "fire meat" tacos are sure to become one of your new favorites.*

Makes 16 tacos (about 5 cups beef)
Total time: 30 minutes + marinating

**PURÉE:**

| | |
|---|---|
| 1 | can pear nectar (11.3 oz.) *or* 1 1/2 cups |
| 3/4 | cup low-sodium soy sauce |
| 1/2 | cup packed brown sugar |
| 1/2 | cup sliced scallions |
| 1/4 | cup *each* dry sherry and rice vinegar |
| 3 | Tbsp. toasted sesame oil |
| 2 | Tbsp. *each* minced fresh garlic and ginger |

**ADD:**

| | |
|---|---|
| 1 | flank steak (1 1/2–2 lb.), thinly sliced |
| 16 | flour tortillas (6-inch) Gochujang to taste Kimchi Toasted sesame seeds |

**Purée** nectar, soy sauce, brown sugar, scallions, sherry, vinegar, oil, garlic, and ginger in a blender or food processor for the marinade.

**Add** steak to a baking dish, then pour marinade over steak. Cover dish and chill 6 hours, or overnight. Discard marinade; pat steak dry.

**Preheat** double-burner grill pan or grill over high. Brush grill pan with oil.

**Grill** steak, in batches, until charred, 1 minute per side. Serve steak on tortillas with gochujang, kimchi, and sesame seeds.

Per taco: 257 cal; 9g total fat (3g sat); 32mg chol; 752mg sodium; 28g carb; (1g fiber, 11g total sugars); 15g protein

**STAFF FAVORITE**

These are Pam's favorite tacos — she's a huge fan of Korean flavors. Check out **CuisineAtHome.com** for more Korean recipes.

## PORK & SHIITAKE MUSHROOM CONGEE

*Leftover congee can be kept in the refrigerator for up to 5 days. Warm on the stove top or in the microwave, and stir in a little extra liquid to loosen it up, if needed.*

Makes 4 servings (4 cups rice)
Total time: 1¼ hours

### HEAT:

| | |
|---|---|
| 8 | cups low-sodium chicken broth |
| 1 | cup jasmine *or* basmati rice |
| ½ | tsp. kosher salt |
| 2 | eggs, beaten |

### MEANWHILE, COOK:

| | |
|---|---|
| 8 | oz. shiitake mushrooms, stemmed and chopped |
| 2 | Tbsp. *each* minced fresh ginger and garlic |
| 2 | Tbsp. olive oil |
| 1 | lb. ground pork |
| ¼ | cup low-sodium soy sauce |

### TOP:

| | |
|---|---|
| 1 | cup finely diced red onions |
| 1 | cup fresh cilantro leaves Sesame-flavored chili oil, *optional* |

**Heat** broth, rice, and salt in a saucepan over medium-high to a boil. Reduce heat to low and simmer, stirring occasionally, until rice is thick and creamy, about 1 hour. Stir 1 cup rice into beaten eggs in a bowl, then stir back into pan.

**Meanwhile, cook** mushrooms, ginger, and garlic in olive oil in a skillet over medium heat (once rice has cooked 45 minutes) until fragrant, 1–2 minutes. Add pork and cook until browned, 10 minutes, crushing with a potato masher until fine. Deglaze skillet with soy sauce, scraping up any brown bits, then cook pork until crispy, 5 minutes more.

**Top** rice with pork mixture, onions, and cilantro; drizzle with chili oil.

Per serving: 642 cal; 34g total fat (11g sat); 175mg chol; 1064mg sodium; 49g carb (3g fiber, 3g total sugars); 32g protein

STAFF
FAVORITE

Haley loves a cheesy casserole, but it's the side dish with this one that she really can't get enough of. It's all of her favorite things combined into one flavorful salad.

## TEX-MEX LASAGNA

*Ancho chile powder gives this casserole deep Tex-Mex flavor. Don't confuse it with chili powder, which can have up to seven spices other than chiles.*

Makes 8 servings
Total time: 1¼ hours

**ARRANGE:**

| | |
|---|---|
| 14 | corn tortillas (6-inch), cut into thirds |

**MELT:**

| | |
|---|---|
| 4 | Tbsp. unsalted butter |
| 1 | cup diced onions |
| 1 | cup diced red bell peppers |
| 1 | large poblano chile, diced |
| 1 | cup frozen corn kernels |
| 2 | Tbsp. minced fresh garlic |

**STIR IN:**

| | |
|---|---|
| ¼ | cup all-purpose flour |
| 2 | Tbsp. ancho chile powder |
| 2 | tsp. ground cumin |
| 1 | tsp. ground coriander |
| 2½ | cups low-sodium chicken broth |
| 1 | Tbsp. fresh lime juice |
| | Salt and black pepper to taste |

**LINE:**

| | |
|---|---|
| 3 | cups cubed rotisserie chicken |
| 8 | oz. Cheddar, shredded |
| 8 | oz. pepper Jack cheese, shredded |

**Preheat** oven to 350°. Lightly coat a 9×13-inch baking dish with nonstick spray.

**Arrange** tortillas in a single layer on two baking sheets. Bake tortillas until slightly crisp, about 15 minutes.
**Melt** butter in a sauté pan over medium-high heat; add onions, bell peppers, poblano, corn, and garlic and cook until softened, 3–4 minutes.
**Stir in** flour, chile powder, cumin, and coriander, then whisk in broth. Bring mixture to a boil and cook until thick, stirring occasionally, about 10 minutes; add lime juice and season with salt and black pepper.
**Line** bottom of prepared baking dish with one-third of the tortilla strips. Layer with one-third of the chicken, vegetable mixture, and cheeses. Repeat twice, using one-third of the ingredients in each layer, ending with cheese.
**Bake** casserole until cheese is bubbly and melted, 30–35 minutes. Let casserole sit 15 minutes before serving.

Per serving: 500 cal; 28g total fat (16g sat); 111mg chol; 516mg sodium; 26g carb (4g fiber, 5g total sugars); 33g protein

Baking the tortillas first brings out the corn flavor and keeps them from getting soggy.

## AVOCADO-LETTUCE SALAD

*If you like both guacamole and crunchy lettuce salads, this creative side dish offers the best of both worlds.*

Makes 8 cups
Total time: 20 minutes

| | |
|---|---|
| 1 | lb. bacon, diced |
| 4 | avocados |
| 6 | Tbsp. mayonnaise |
| ¼ | cup *each* fresh lime and lemon juice |
| | Salt and black pepper to taste |
| 8 | cups shredded iceberg lettuce |
| 4 | Roma tomatoes, seeded and diced |
| ⅔ | cup sliced scallions |
| ⅔ | cup chopped fresh cilantro |
| ¼ | cup seeded, minced jalapeño |

**Cook** bacon in a skillet until crisp; transfer to a paper-towel-lined plate.
**Mash** avocados in a large bowl until smooth; add mayonnaise, lime juice, and lemon juice; season with salt and black pepper.
**Stir** lettuce, tomatoes, scallions, cilantro, jalapeño, and bacon into avocado mixture until combined.

Per ½ cup: 243 cal; 22g total fat (5g sat); 21mg chol; 230mg sodium; 7g carb (4g fiber, 2g total sugars); 5g protein

33

**STAFF FAVORITE**

Not everyone eats mussels on staff, but Pam and Kim can't get enough of them. Based on a French classic, mussels and fries, this menu breaks away from tradition by serving up crouton fries instead.

## ROSÉ WINE-STEAMED MUSSELS

*You'll be hard-pressed to decide which element you like better — the rosé wine and fennel broth or the tender mussels.*

Makes 6 servings
Total time: 35 minutes

**HEAT:**

2      Tbsp. olive oil
1      fennel bulb (about 10 oz.), trimmed and thinly sliced (about 2 cups)
1/3    cup minced shallots
2      Tbsp. minced fresh garlic

**ADD:**

1      bottle dry rosé wine (750 ml)
3      lb. mussels, scrubbed and debearded

**OFF HEAT, SWIRL:**

4      Tbsp. unsalted butter, cubed and softened
1 1/2  tsp. minced fresh thyme
       Salt and black pepper to taste
       Chopped fennel fronds

**Heat** oil in a large pot over medium-low. Add fennel, shallots, and garlic; cook until softened, 5–7 minutes.

**Add** wine and increase heat to high; bring to a boil and reduce wine to 2 cups, about 5 minutes. (If wine measures less than 2 cups add more rosé to equal 2 cups.)

**Add** mussels, cover, and cook, shaking pot occasionally, until mussels open, about 5 minutes. Discard any mussels that don't open. Using a slotted spoon, divide mussels among six bowls.

**Off heat, swirl** butter into the broth until melted; stir in thyme and season with salt and pepper. Divide broth among bowls and top with fennel fronds.

Per serving: 387 cal; 17g total fat (6g sat); 84mg chol; 669mg sodium; 15g carb (1g fiber, 2g total sugars); 28g protein

Once you've trimmed the stalks and root end, slice the fennel bulb in half, then remove the center core.

To determine if wine is reduced enough, strain it and solids through a sieve set over a measuring cup.

Don't get hung up on cutting your fries the perfect size — some will be larger and others a tad smaller.

## CROUTON FRIES

*These "fries" are one of those foods that once you start eating, you won't be able to stop.*

Makes 6 servings
Total time: 30 minutes

**COMBINE:**

1      tsp. kosher salt
1/2    tsp. black pepper
1/2    tsp. granulated garlic

**HEAT:**

1      cup olive oil, divided
4      Tbsp. unsalted butter, divided
1      Italian baguette, sliced into 3 x 3/4-inch sticks

**Preheat** oven to 200°. Line a baking sheet with paper towels.

**Combine** salt, pepper, and garlic.

**Heat** 1/4 cup oil and 1 Tbsp. butter in a large cast-iron skillet over medium-high until butter melts. Add a quarter of the bread sticks and sauté, turning often, until all sides are toasted.

**Transfer** Crouton Fries to prepared baking sheet to drain; season with 1/2 tsp. salt mixture, then transfer to oven to keep warm. Repeat procedure 3 more times with remaining oil, butter, salt mixture, and bread sticks.

Per serving: 431 cal; 36g total fat (9g sat); 20mg chol; 578mg sodium; 25g carb (0g fiber, 0g total sugars); 4g protein

ALL-TIME **FAVORITES**

## SESAME-CRUSTED SALMON WITH WASABI DIPPING SAUCE

*Wasabi paste is a ready-to-use mixture of dried horseradish, mustard, food coloring, and water. You can find it in most grocery stores.*

Makes 4 servings
Total time: 30 minutes

**FOR THE SAUCE, WHISK:**

| | |
|---|---|
| ¼ | cup low-sodium soy sauce |
| 1 | Tbsp. rice vinegar |
| 2 | tsp. wasabi paste (such as S&B) |
| 1 | tsp. honey |
| 1 | Tbsp. minced scallions |

**FOR THE SALMON, COMBINE:**

| | |
|---|---|
| 1 | Tbsp. *each* black and toasted white sesame seeds |
| 4 | salmon fillets (5 oz. *each*), skin removed |
| 1 | Tbsp. canola oil |

**Preheat** oven to 450° with rack in top third.

**For the sauce, whisk** together soy sauce, vinegar, wasabi paste, and honey; stir in scallions.

**For the salmon, combine** black and white sesame seeds. Coat salmon with nonstick spray and top with sesame seeds.

**Heat** oil in an ovenproof nonstick skillet over medium-high. Add salmon, seed sides up; cook until bottom is crisp, 5 minutes. Transfer skillet to top rack of oven and roast salmon to desired doneness, or until a thermometer inserted into salmon registers 140° for medium-well, 3–4 minutes more. Serve salmon with sauce.

Per serving: 253 cal; 11g total fat (1g sat); 72mg chol; 741mg sodium; 4g carb (0g fiber, 1g total sugars); 33g protein

# SPICY BEEF FRIED RICE

Makes 6 servings (8 cups)
Total time: 30 minutes

**HEAT:**

| | |
|---|---|
| 3 | Tbsp. vegetable oil, divided |
| 3 | eggs, lightly beaten |

**ADD:**

| | |
|---|---|
| 1 | pkg. frozen classic mixed vegetables (16 oz.) |
| 1/4 | cup minced scallion whites and light greens |
| 1 | Tbsp. *each* minced fresh garlic and ginger |
| 1 | lb. flank steak, thinly sliced, seasoned with salt and black pepper |

**STIR IN:**

| | |
|---|---|
| 1/4 | cup low-sodium soy sauce |
| 1 | Tbsp. *each* sambal oelek and sesame oil |
| 1 1/2 | cups long-grain rice, cooked and chilled |
| 1/2 | cup sliced scallion greens |

**Heat** 1 Tbsp. vegetable oil in a wok or large skillet over medium-high, swirling to coat pan. Add eggs, swirl pan so eggs form a large thin pancake; cook until eggs are set. Loosen egg with a spatula and transfer to a plate to cool.

**Add** 1 Tbsp. vegetable oil to wok and increase heat to high. Add frozen vegetables and stir-fry until softened, 3–5 minutes. Stir in scallion whites and light greens, garlic, and ginger; cook until fragrant, 1 minute, then transfer to plate with eggs.

**Add** remaining 1 Tbsp. vegetable oil to wok; add steak and stir-fry until browned on both sides, 2–3 minutes.

**Stir in** soy sauce, sambal oelek, and sesame oil. Stir in rice, scallion greens, and egg until heated through.

Per serving: 349 cal; 17g total fat (4g sat); 142mg chol; 534mg sodium; 24g carb (2g fiber, 4g total sugars); 23g protein

**STAFF FAVORITE**

The combination of beef and spice is what Chris likes so much about this recipe, plus it's so simple to prepare.

## CAST-IRON SKILLETS

An indispensable piece of cookware, cast-iron gets its name from the way it's made. Molten iron is "cast" in a mold made of sand. The outcome is a skillet with a porous surface that needs to be "seasoned" before using.

## CHICKEN TAMALE PIE

*If you love tamales but don't want to mess around with corn husks and fussy assembly, this tamale baked in a skillet will be right up your alley.*

Makes 6 servings (one 10-inch pie)
Total time: 1 hour

**PULSE:**

3 cups chopped fresh tomatoes, divided
1/2 cup diced onion
2 cloves garlic, smashed

**HEAT:**

1 Tbsp. olive oil
2 Tbsp. chili powder
1 Tbsp. all-purpose flour
2 tsp. ground cumin
1 cup low-sodium chicken broth
2 cups shredded cooked chicken
   Salt and black pepper to taste

**COMBINE:**

3/4 cup yellow cornmeal
1/2 cup all-purpose flour
11/2 tsp. *each* baking powder and sugar
1 tsp. table salt
1 egg
3/4 cup buttermilk
2 Tbsp. unsalted butter, melted
1 cup frozen corn kernels, thawed
1 can diced green chiles (4.5 oz.), drained
1 Tbsp. unsalted butter
2 cups shredded Colby Jack cheese

**Preheat** oven to 425°. Place a 10-inch cast-iron skillet on a baking sheet and transfer to the oven.

**Pulse** 2 cups tomatoes, onion, and garlic in a food processor until nearly puréed.

**Heat** oil in a saucepan over medium. Stir in chili powder, 1 Tbsp. flour, and cumin; cook 1 minute. Whisk in broth and tomato mixture; bring to a boil. Reduce heat to medium-low and simmer sauce until thickened, 10 minutes, stirring occasionally. Season sauce with salt and pepper, then cool. Reserve 1/2 cup sauce, then stir in chicken and remaining 1 cup tomatoes.

**Combine** cornmeal, 1/2 cup flour, baking powder, sugar, and 1 tsp. salt.

**Whisk** together egg, buttermilk, and melted butter. Fold in dry ingredients just until combined, then stir in corn and green chiles.

**Melt** 1 Tbsp. butter in preheated skillet; carefully add batter and bake 20 minutes. Poke holes in cornbread; spread reserved 1/2 cup sauce over top. Add chicken mixture, sprinkle with cheese, and bake pie 10 minutes.

Per serving: 490 cal; 22g total fat (12g sat); 122mg chol; 948mg sodium; 42g carb (2g fiber, 3g total sugars); 30g protein

## PINTO BEAN SALAD WITH LEMON-GARLIC VINAIGRETTE

Makes 6 servings (about 4 cups)
Total time: 20 minutes

**COMBINE:**

1 can pinto beans (16 oz.), drained and rinsed
1 cup frozen corn kernels, thawed
1 cup halved and thinly sliced radishes
3/4 cup sliced scallions

**CRUSH:**

1 Tbsp. chopped fresh garlic
1/4 tsp. kosher salt

**WHISK:**

1 Tbsp. minced lemon zest
2 Tbsp. fresh lemon juice
1 Tbsp. olive oil
   Salt and black pepper to taste

**Combine** beans, corn, radishes, and scallions.

**Crush** garlic on a cutting board; top garlic with 1/4 tsp. salt, then press and drag with the flat side of knife blade until a paste forms.

**Whisk** together zest, lemon juice, oil, and garlic paste; toss with bean mixture. Season salad with salt and pepper and chill until ready to serve.

Per serving: 135 cal; 3g total fat (0g sat); 0mg chol; 263mg sodium; 21g carb (1g fiber, 2g total sugars); 6g protein

For the ideal texture, pulse the tomatoes, onions, and garlic until nearly puréed.

To prevent overmixing the cornbread batter, fold the dry ingredients into the wet ones.

## SHRIMP & GRITS WITH TOMATO CREAM SAUCE

Makes 4 servings
(3 cups shrimp, 2 cups sauce)
Total time: 25 minutes

| | |
|---|---|
| 2 | Tbsp. unsalted butter, divided |
| 1½ | cups diced tomatoes |
| ½ | cup heavy cream |
| ¼ | cup low-sodium chicken broth |
| ½ | cup chopped scallion greens |
| 3 | Tbsp. dry sherry, divided |
| 1 | cup ½-inch-thick slices kielbasa |
| ¼ | cup diced onion |
| ¼ | cup *each* diced red and yellow bell pepper |
| 1 | Tbsp. minced fresh garlic |
| 16 | large shrimp, peeled and deveined (tails left on) |
| 2 | tsp. Old Bay seasoning |
| ½ | tsp. *each* cayenne pepper, kosher salt, and black pepper |
| | Chopped scallion greens |

**Melt** 1 Tbsp. butter in a saucepan over medium-high heat for the sauce. Add tomatoes and sauté 2 minutes, then add cream and broth. Reduce heat to medium-low and simmer sauce 5 minutes.

**Stir in** ½ cup scallion greens and 1 Tbsp. sherry, season sauce with salt and black pepper, and simmer 3 minutes. Keep sauce warm over very low heat.

**Melt** remaining 1 Tbsp. butter in a nonstick skillet over medium heat; add kielbasa and sauté 1 minute. Add onion, bell pepper, and garlic; sauté until onion softens, about 4 minutes.

**Season** shrimp with Old Bay, cayenne, salt, and black pepper, then add to kielbasa. Sauté shrimp until fully cooked, 3 minutes. Deglaze skillet with remaining 2 Tbsp. sherry; cook until sherry evaporates, 1 minute.

**Divide** grits, *right*, sauce, and shrimp among four bowls, then top with scallions.

Per serving: 245cal; 19g total fat (11g sat); 90mg chol; 495mg sodium; 8g carb (2g fiber, 4g total sugars); 7g protein

## CUISINE POKE BOWL

*Be sure to choose fish labeled as "previously frozen." This ensures the fish has been frozen to below -4°F, which according to FDA guidelines, is a sufficient temperature to kill parasites.*

Makes 4 servings
Total time: 30 minutes

| | |
|---|---|
| ⅓ | cup ponzu |
| 4 | tsp. honey |
| 1 | Tbsp. toasted sesame oil |
| 2 | tsp. sesame seeds, toasted Himalayan pink salt to taste |
| 1 | lb. salmon, skin removed, cut into ¾-inch cubes |
| 3 | cups cooked brown jasmine rice |
| 1 | avocado, sliced |
| 1 | cup frozen shelled edamame, blanched |
| 4 | radishes, thinly sliced |
| 1 | small sweet yellow onion (such as Maui), thinly sliced |
| ½ | cup pickled ginger |
| ¼ | cup furikake |

**Combine** ponzu, honey, sesame oil, and sesame seeds in a bowl for the sauce; season with salt. Add salmon, toss to coat, cover, and chill until ready to serve.

**Divide** rice, salmon (reserve sauce), avocado, edamame, radishes, onion, and ginger among bowls.

**Drizzle** reserved sauce over bowls and sprinkle with furikake.

Per serving: 561cal; 22g total fat (2g sat); 58mg chol; 1392mg sodium; 58g carb (9g fiber, 11g total sugars); 36g protein

# CREAMY GRITS

**Makes 4 servings (3 cups)**
**Total time: 25 minutes**

Prepare 1 cup white or yellow grits according to package directions (use equal parts milk and water for the liquid). Season grits to taste with salt and black pepper and keep warm. Top each serving with 1 tsp. butter.

**STAFF FAVORITE**

If Teresa had one last meal, it would have to include shrimp, and this recipe is a front-runner.

# TOFU STIR-FRY WITH BLACK PEPPER SAUCE

Makes 2 servings
Total time: 40 minutes

## CUT:
- 1 pkg. extra-firm tofu (14 oz.), blotted dry
- 1/4 cup cornstarch
- 1/2 tsp. kosher salt
- 1 1/2 cups vegetable oil

## WHISK:
- 1/3 cup low-sodium vegetable broth
- 2 Tbsp. *each* low-sodium soy sauce, sweet soy sauce, and oyster sauce
- 2 Tbsp. light brown sugar
- 2 tsp. cornstarch
- 2 tsp. coarsely ground black pepper
- 1/8 tsp. white pepper

## STIR-FRY:
- 1 1/2 cups thinly sliced shallots
- 2 Tbsp. minced red bell pepper
- 6 scallions, cut into 1-inch bias-sliced pieces
- 1 Tbsp. *each* minced fresh garlic and ginger
- 1/4 tsp. red pepper flakes
  Cooked jasmine rice
  Bias-sliced scallion greens

**Cut** tofu into 1-inch cubes. Whisk together 1/4 cup cornstarch and salt; add tofu and toss to coat.

**Heat** oil in a sauté pan or wok over medium-high. Shake off excess cornstarch, add tofu to pan, and fry until crisp and browned on all sides, 4–5 minutes. Transfer tofu to a paper-towel-lined plate. Discard all but 1 Tbsp. oil in pan.

**Whisk** together broth, low-sodium soy sauce, sweet soy sauce, oyster sauce, brown sugar, 2 tsp. cornstarch, black pepper, and white pepper for the sauce.

**Stir-fry** shallots and bell pepper in oil in same pan over medium-high heat until softened, 3–5 minutes. Add scallion pieces, garlic, ginger, and pepper flakes; stir-fry until fragrant, 1–2 minutes. Add tofu and broth mixture, stirring to coat; cook until thickened.

**Serve** stir-fry with rice and top with scallion greens.

Per serving: 554 cal; 18g total fat (1g sat); 0mg chol; 1595mg sodium; 80g carb (9g fiber, 23g total sugars); 23g protein

## CUBAN BLACK BEANS & QUINOA

*Cooked in half the time of brown rice, and full of iron and potassium, quinoa brings something more to the table in this slightly spicy dish.*

Makes 4 servings
Total time: 30 minutes

**FOR THE QUINOA, HEAT:**

| | |
|---|---|
| 2 | tsp. vegetable *or* canola oil |
| 1 | cup quinoa |
| 1 | tsp. minced fresh garlic |
| 1 | cup *each* low-sodium vegetable broth and water |
| 1 | dried bay leaf |

**FOR THE BEANS, HEAT:**

| | |
|---|---|
| 2 | tsp. vegetable *or* canola oil |
| 1/2 | cup diced red onion |
| 1 | Tbsp. minced fresh garlic |
| 2 | tsp. *each* ground cumin and dried oregano |
| 1/4 | tsp. cayenne pepper |

**DEGLAZE:**

| | |
|---|---|
| 2 | Tbsp. distilled white vinegar |

**PURÉE:**

| | |
|---|---|
| 2 | cans reduced-sodium black beans (15 oz. *each*), drained and rinsed |
| 1/2 | cup water |

**FOR THE PICO, COMBINE:**

| | |
|---|---|
| 1/2 | cup diced grape tomatoes |
| 1/4 | cup *each* minced jalapeño and red onion |
| | Lime wedges |

**STAFF FAVORITE**

Kim tries to eat a plant-based diet at home, and with recipes like this one, it's easy to do.

**For the quinoa, heat** oil in a saucepan over medium-high. Add quinoa and garlic; cook 1 minute. Stir in broth, water, and bay leaf; bring to a boil. Reduce heat to low, cover, and cook quinoa until liquid is absorbed, 15–20 minutes.

**For the beans, heat** oil in a skillet over medium. Add red onion, garlic, cumin, oregano, and cayenne; cook until onion softens, 2–3 minutes.

**Deglaze** skillet with vinegar, scraping up any brown bits, and reduce until vinegar is nearly absorbed.

**Purée** half the beans in a food processor and stir back into skillet along with remaining whole beans and water until combined and heated through, 2 minutes.

**For the pico, combine** tomatoes, jalapeño, and red onion. Serve quinoa with beans, pico, and limes.

Per serving: 403 cal; 8g total fat (1g sat); 0mg chol; 333mg sodium; 69g carb (19g fiber, 5g total sugars); 18g protein

## CHICKEN ENCHILADAS

*Rotisserie chicken makes these enchiladas especially quick and flavor-packed, but you can use any cooked chicken.*

Makes 8 enchiladas (2½ cups sauce)
Total time: 1 hour

**FOR THE SAUCE, PURÉE:**
- 1    can diced tomatoes in juice (14.5 oz.)
- ½    cup chopped onion
- 1    Tbsp. chopped fresh garlic

**HEAT:**
- 2    Tbsp. olive oil
- 1    Tbsp. all-purpose flour
- 2    Tbsp. chili powder
- 2    tsp. ground cumin
- 1    cup low-sodium chicken broth
      Salt and black pepper to taste

**FOR THE FILLING, COMBINE:**
- 2    cups shredded cooked chicken
- 1    can diced tomatoes (14.5 oz.), drained
- ½    cup diced onion
- 2    cups shredded Cheddar, divided
- 8    flour tortillas (8-inch)

**Preheat** oven to 350°.

**For the sauce, purée** tomatoes, onion, and garlic in a food processor.

**Heat** oil in a large saucepan over medium. Stir in flour, chili powder, and cumin; cook 1 minute. Whisk in puréed tomato mixture and broth; bring to a boil. Reduce heat to medium-low and simmer sauce until thickened, 15–20 minutes, stirring occasionally. Season sauce with salt and pepper and let cool.

**For the filling, combine** chicken, tomatoes, onion, 1 cup Cheddar, and ½ cup sauce.

**Spread** ½ cup sauce in bottom of a 9x13-inch baking dish. Place 1 tortilla into dish, spread on 1 Tbsp. sauce, and flip.

**Scoop** 2 Tbsp. filling onto tortilla, and roll to enclose; arrange, seam side down, in the dish. Repeat saucing, filling, and rolling with remaining tortillas.

**Top** enchiladas with remaining sauce and 1 cup Cheddar. Bake enchiladas until Cheddar melts and sauce is bubbly, 30 minutes; let cool slightly before serving.

Per enchilada: 388 cal; 17g total fat (8g sat); 60mg chol; 947mg sodium; 35g carb (4g fiber, 5g total sugars); 23g protein

**STAFF FAVORITE**

Maddy's family is crazy about Mexican food, and this is one recipe that's served frequently.

# MUFFULETTA DUTCH BABY

Makes 4 servings
Total time: 30 minutes

**COMBINE:**

3/4 cup all-purpose flour

1/2 tsp. kosher salt

1/4 tsp. *each* red pepper flakes
and black pepper

**WHISK:**

4 eggs, room temperature

3/4 cup whole milk, room
temperature

1 tsp. Dijon mustard

1 cup shredded provolone
(4 oz.), divided

2 Tbsp. unsalted butter

3 oz. *each* thinly sliced salami
and deli ham

1/3 cup chopped fresh tomatoes
Chopped fresh parsley

**Preheat** oven to 425° with an
8-inch cast-iron skillet on the
center rack.

**Combine** flour, salt, pepper flakes,
and black pepper in a bowl.

**Whisk** together eggs, milk, and
Dijon. Whisk egg mixture into
flour mixture until combined;
stir in 1/2 cup provolone.

**Remove** skillet from oven and
add butter, swirling to coat bottom
and sides. Layer half the salami
and ham in bottom of skillet;
pour egg mixture over meat.

**Bake** Dutch baby until puffed
and golden brown around edges
(center will still be custardy),
16–18 minutes. Remove skillet
from oven. Preheat broiler with
rack 6-inches from element.

**Layer** remaining salami and
ham over Dutch baby; top with
remaining 1/2 cup provolone
and broil until cheese melts,
2 minutes.

**Top** Dutch baby with tomatoes
and parsley.

Per serving: 435 cal; 27g total fat (13g sat);
260mg chol; 1141mg sodium; 22g carb (1g fiber,
4g total sugars); 26g protein

**STAFF FAVORITE**

Classic New Orleans
sandwich meets Dutch
baby in this food fusion
that Chris is wild about.

**STAFF FAVORITE**

Teresa likes to serve these medallions when she entertains. The flavors of lemon, rosemary, and garlic elevate the dish.

## PROSCIUTTO-WRAPPED PORK MEDALLIONS WITH FIORENTINA SAUCE

*Based on one of Tuscany's most celebrated dishes — Bistecca alla Fiorentina — this pork version will be praised, too.*

Makes 4 servings
Total time: 30 minutes

### FOR THE SAUCE, COMBINE:

| | |
|---|---|
| 1/3 | cup olive oil |
| 1 | Tbsp. fresh lemon juice |
| 1 | Tbsp. minced fresh sage |
| 2 | tsp. minced fresh rosemary |
| 2 | tsp. minced fresh garlic |
| 2 | tsp. minced lemon zest |
| | Salt and red pepper flakes to taste |

### FOR THE PORK, COAT:

| | |
|---|---|
| 1 1/2 | lb. pork tenderloin, trimmed of fat and silverskin, sliced into 2 1/2-inch-thick medallions (5–6 oz. *each*) |
| | Olive oil |
| | Black pepper |
| 4 | slices prosciutto, folded in half horizontally |

**Preheat** grill to medium-high. Brush grill grate with oil.

**For the sauce, combine** oil, lemon juice, sage, rosemary, garlic, and zest; season with salt and pepper flakes; pour into a shallow dish.

**For the pork, coat** medallions with oil; season with salt and black pepper. Wrap a slice of prosciutto around each medallion and secure with kitchen string.

**Grill** medallions, covered, until a thermometer inserted into centers registers 145°, about 5 minutes per side.

**Transfer** medallions to prepared dish, flip in sauce, and let rest 3–4 minutes, flipping frequently. Remove strings from medallions; serve with sauce.

Per serving: 388 cal; 24g total fat (4g sat); 122mg chol; 466mg sodium; 2g carb (0g fiber, 0g total sugars); 40g protein

## THREE-HERB FALAFEL WITH TAHINI SAUCE

Makes 6 servings (about 2 dozen falafel)
Total time: about 1 hour + soaking

### FOR THE SAUCE, PURÉE:

- 3/4 cup tahini
- 1/3 cup *each* fresh lemon juice and water
- 1 1/2 tsp. minced fresh garlic
- 1 tsp. kosher salt
- 1/4 tsp. cayenne pepper

### FOR THE FALAFEL, PULSE:

- 1 1/2 cups dried chickpeas (about 10.5 oz.), soaked 12–24 hours, drained, rinsed, and patted dry
- 1 medium red onion, chopped (about 1 1/4 cups)
- 1/3 cup *each* chopped fresh cilantro, mint, and parsley
- 3 Tbsp. all-purpose flour
- 1/2 jalapeño, seeded and minced (about 3 Tbsp.)
- 1 Tbsp. minced fresh garlic
- 1 Tbsp. kosher salt
- 1 1/2 tsp. *each* ground cumin and coriander
- 1 tsp. baking powder
- 1/4 tsp. black pepper

### HEAT:

Canola *or* vegetable oil
- 6 flatbreads (7-inch)
Sliced romaine lettuce, sliced red onion, seeded and sliced cucumber, and halved grape tomatoes

**For the sauce, purée** tahini, lemon juice, water, garlic, salt, and cayenne in a mini food processor. (Sauce can be made ahead and chilled, but bring to room temperature before serving.)

**For the falafel, pulse** chickpeas, chopped red onion, cilantro, mint, parsley, flour, jalapeño, garlic, salt, cumin, coriander, baking powder, and black pepper in a food processor until minced and crumbly, scraping down sides as necessary.

**Scoop** dough with a #40 scoop (1 1/2 Tbsp.); roll into ping-pong-sized balls, pressing firmly.

**Heat** a large pot filled two-thirds full with oil to 350°. Line a baking sheet with paper towels.

**Fry** falafel in four batches until golden brown, gently nudging so they don't stick to the bottom, about 4 minutes per batch; transfer to prepared baking sheet.

**Top** flatbreads with lettuce, sliced onion, cucumber, tomatoes, falafel, and sauce.

Per serving: 653 cal; 31g total fat (33g sat); 0mg chol; 1716mg sodium; 77g carb (14g fiber, 8g total sugars); 22g protein

47

FIRED UP FOR
# FRIED
# CHICKEN

We play a game here at Cuisine: "What would be your last meal?" While our roots vary, we all pretty much share the same wish — that our final meal be SOUTHERN FRIED CHICKEN. With a crisp golden crust and moist, tender meat flavored simply with lots of salt and pepper, it's a favorite around here.

## CLASSIC SOUTHERN FRIED CHICKEN

*It's best to fry chicken in a cast-iron skillet with a tight-fitting lid. The lid is crucial — the chicken steams as it fries for super-moist results.*

Makes 5 servings (10 pieces)
Total time: 30 minutes

**SOAK:**
1   whole chicken (3–4 lb.), cut into 10 pieces
1   cup buttermilk
    Salt and black pepper

**COMBINE:**
2   cups all-purpose flour
1   Tbsp. kosher salt
1   Tbsp. black pepper

**HEAT:**
2   cups peanut oil

**Soak** chicken pieces in buttermilk for 20 minutes, then place them on a baking sheet lined with a rack. Season chicken on both sides with salt and pepper.

**Combine** flour, 1 Tbsp. salt, and 1 Tbsp. pepper in a large paper bag. Dredge chicken in flour, shake off excess, and return pieces to rack.

**Heat** oil in a large cast-iron skillet over medium-high to 360°. Add a few chicken pieces, skin sides down, reduce heat to medium, and fry until brown, 6–8 minutes. Flip chicken, reduce heat to low, cover, and fry until a thermometer inserted into the thickest part, but not touching bone, registers 165°, about 10 minutes. Uncover skillet and fry chicken to crisp the coating, 3–4 minutes more.

**Transfer** chicken to a paper-towel-lined baking sheet to drain, 10 minutes, before serving. Repeat frying with remaining chicken.

**Reserve** 1/4 cup oil in skillet for the Chunky Tomato Gravy, *page 50.*

Per serving: 869 calories; 59g total fat (16g sat); 239mg chol; 1387mg sodium; 19g carb (1g fiber, 1g total sugars); 62g protein

**3 STEPS TO FRIED CHICKEN SUCCESS**

Massage buttermilk into the crevices of the chicken to coat it thoroughly. Then let it soak at room temperature.

Don't crowd the skillet — leave a little space between the chicken pieces so the oil adequately surrounds them.

Insert a thermometer into the thickest part of each piece. The chicken is fully cooked through at 165°.

**STAFF FAVORITE**

The entire Cuisine staff adores a good fried chicken dinner. And this Southern interpretation, made with tomato gravy, collards and rice, and the best sweet tea ever, is one for the record books!

Popular in the South, TOMATO GRAVY is colorful and sharp-tasting, and oh-so-good with fried chicken. The thickness of the gravy is a matter of preference, so at any time during cooking, you can thin it out with chicken broth or water. Spoon this gravy over rice and greens, biscuits, or even a big bowl of grits!

**ONLINE EXTRA**
If this Tomato Gravy isn't your thing, try the Milk Gravy recipe at CuisineAtHome.com.

**TO ACHIEVE GRAVY SUCCESS**, ONCE THE LIQUIDS ARE ADDED, IT WON'T TAKE LONG FOR THE GRAVY TO THICKEN. BUT STIR IT OFTEN TO KEEP IT FROM SCORCHING.

## CHUNKY TOMATO GRAVY

Makes 6 servings (3 cups)
Total time: 15 minutes

| | |
|---|---|
| 1 | cup diced onions |
| ¼ | cup oil (from pan drippings) |
| ¼ | cup all-purpose flour |
| 2 | cups Roma tomatoes, chopped and pulsed in a food processor |
| 1 | cup whole milk |
| ½ | cup low-sodium chicken broth |
| 2 | tsp. cider vinegar |
| | Salt and black pepper to taste |

**Sauté** onions in oil in a saucepan over medium-high heat until soft, about 3 minutes. Stir in flour and cook until lightly golden, about 2 minutes.

**Add** tomatoes to pan and sauté 1 minute. Stir in milk, broth, and vinegar; cook until slightly thickened, 4–5 minutes. Season gravy with salt and pepper.

Per serving: 150 calories; 11g total fat (2g sat); 4mg chol; 27mg sodium; 11g carb (1g fiber, 5g total sugars); 3g protein

"This is one delicious dinner, but to make a good thing even better, go to our website for our Basic Buttermilk Biscuits recipe."

**Robin Zimmerman**
Senior Test Kitchen Associate

FOR COLOR, FLAVOR, AND TRADITION ADD CHOPPED COLLARD GREENS (OR ANY OTHER GREEN, LIKE SPINACH). SPRINKLE THE GREENS WITH SALT SO THEY WILT A BIT.

## RICE PILAF WITH COLLARDS

*To stem and chop greens, fold each leaf in half lengthwise and trim out the stem. Slice the leaf into 1/2-inch wide strips, then chop into smaller pieces.*

Makes 6 servings (3 cups)
Total time: 35 minutes

3   cups stemmed and chopped collard greens
1 1/2   tsp. kosher salt, divided
2   Tbsp. unsalted butter
1   cup diced onions
1   tsp. minced lemon zest
1   cup converted rice
2   cups low-sodium chicken broth
1   dried bay leaf

**Toss** collards with 1/2 tsp. salt and let stand while the rice cooks.

**Melt** butter in a saucepan over medium heat. Add onions, zest, and remaining 1 tsp. salt and cook until soft, 2–3 minutes. Stir in rice and cook 1 minute.

**Add** broth and bay leaf; bring to a simmer. Reduce heat to medium-low, cover, and cook until liquid is absorbed, about 15 minutes. Off heat, let stand, covered, 5 minutes.

**Sprinkle** salted collards on top of the rice. Drape a clean towel under the lid (to absorb excess moisture) and let stand 5 minutes more.

**Stir** collards into rice with a fork.

Per serving: 135 calories; 0g total fat (0g sat);

## SOUTHERN SWEET TEA WITH LIME & MINT

*Refreshing and refined, sweet tea is the American South's thirst quencher of choice. This is pure pleasure in a glass.*

Makes 12 cups
Total time: 10 minutes

12   cups water, divided
1   gallon-size black tea bag
1 1/2   cups sugar
        Lime rounds or wedges
        Sprigs of fresh mint

**Bring** 4 cups water to a boil in a large saucepan. Add tea bag, cover, and steep 5–10 minutes.

**Remove** bag, squeeze dry, then stir in the sugar until dissolved. Add the remaining 8 cups water; chill until cold.

**Serve** tea over ice with limes and mint sprigs.

Per cup: 60 cal; 0g total fat (0g sat); 0mg chol; 0mg sodium; 18g carb (0g fiber, 18g total sugars); 0g protein

ALL-TIME **FAVORITES**

# PECAN-CRUSTED CHICKEN SALAD

Makes 4 servings (7 cups salad,
1¼ cups vinaigrette)
Total time: 40 minutes

**FOR THE VINAIGRETTE, WHISK:**

- ²/₃ cup fresh orange juice
- ¹/₃ cup fresh lemon juice
- ¼ cup olive oil
- 2 Tbsp. honey
- 1 Tbsp. Dijon mustard
  Salt to taste

**FOR THE SALAD, COARSELY CHOP:**

- 1½ cups fresh bread crumbs
- ¾ cup pecans
- 1 tsp. kosher salt
- ½ tsp. cayenne
- 2 Tbsp. *each* lemon and orange zests

**DREDGE:**

- 1¼ lb. boneless, skinless chicken breasts, cut into strips
  All-purpose flour
- 3 eggs
- ¼ cup milk

**HEAT:**

- 2 cups vegetable oil

**TOSS:**

- 1 bag fresh spinach (9 oz.)
- ½ cup thinly sliced red onion
- 4 oz. bacon, diced and cooked
- 4 hard-cooked eggs, cut into wedges

**For the vinaigrette, whisk** together orange and lemon juices, oil, honey, and Dijon; season with salt.

**For the salad, coarsely chop** bread crumbs, pecans, salt, cayenne, and zests in a food processor.

**Dredge** chicken in flour. Whisk eggs and milk together in a shallow dish. Dip floured chicken in egg mixture, then roll in crumb-nut mixture.

**Heat** oil in a large sauté pan over medium to 350°. Fry chicken strips in batches until golden, 2–3 minutes per side; transfer to a paper towel-lined plate.

**Toss** spinach and onion in a bowl with vinaigrette. Top with chicken, bacon, and eggs.

Per serving: 948 calories; 65g total fat (12g sat); 402mg chol; 1029mg sodium; 43g carb (5g fiber, 16g total sugars); 52g protein

# FRIED CHICKEN SANDWICHES

*White Mountain rolls are perfect for this sandwich. Look for them in your grocery store bakery, or large hamburger buns work just as well.*

Makes 4 servings (4 sandwiches)
Total time: 30 minutes + soaking

### POUND:

2    boneless, skinless chicken breasts (8 oz. *each*), halved lengthwise

1    cup buttermilk

1    tsp. Tabasco sauce

### COMBINE:

1    cup all-purpose flour

1/4    cup cornstarch

1    tsp. kosher salt

1/2    tsp. *each* black pepper and cayenne pepper

1/2    cup peanut *or* vegetable oil

4    White Mountain rolls, split, brushed with mayonnaise, and toasted

    Green leaf *or* romaine lettuce

    Kosher dill pickle chips

**Line** a baking sheet with parchment paper and set a rack inside.

**Pound** breast halves into 1/4-inch-thick cutlets with a meat mallet.

**Whisk** together buttermilk and Tabasco in a bowl; add chicken and refrigerate 30 minutes.

**Combine** flour, cornstarch, salt, black pepper, and cayenne in a shallow dish. Remove chicken from buttermilk, letting excess drip off, then dredge in flour mixture and transfer to prepared rack; let stand 10 minutes. Dip chicken in buttermilk again, then back into flour; transfer to prepared rack and let stand 10 minutes more.

**Heat** oil in a 12-inch cast-iron skillet over medium-high to 350°. Fry chicken until golden brown, 2–3 minutes per side. Transfer chicken to a paper-towel-lined baking sheet.

**Serve** chicken on rolls with lettuce, pickles, and rémoulade.

Per serving: 549 cal; 23g total fat (4g sat); 91mg chol; 1551mg sodium; 50g carb (1g fiber, 7g total sugars); 34g protein

## RÉMOULADE WITH PIMENTOS

Combine 1/2 cup mayonnaise, 1 jar sliced pimentos (2 oz.), drained and chopped, 2 Tbsp. *each* chopped shallots, kosher dill pickles, and fresh parsley, 1 Tbsp. *each* capers and fresh lemon juice, and 1 tsp. *each* Dijon mustard and honey; season with salt and black pepper.

Per 2 Tbsp.: 97 cal; 10g total fat (2g sat); 5mg chol; 157mg sodium; 2g carb (0g fiber, 1g total sugars); 0g protein

If you like fried chicken, rice, and "gravy," then this quick-to-fix JAPANESE FRIED CHICKEN meal is for you. Based on a Japanese fast food dish called katsudon [KAHT-soo-dohn], it's one in the "donburi" [dohn-boo-REE] family, which literally means "rice bowls." Once you taste this chicken cutlet, you'll use any excuse in the book to make it again — and again.

# JAPANESE FRIED CHICKEN

*To ensure a crisp crust, be sure to heat the oil before frying the chicken.*

Makes 4 servings
Total time: 45 minutes

**FOR THE SAUCE, SIMMER:**

| | |
|---|---|
| 2 | cups low-sodium chicken broth |
| 2 | cups sliced yellow onions |
| 1/2 | cup *each* mirin and low-sodium soy sauce |
| 2 | Tbsp. minced fresh ginger |
| 1 | Tbsp. minced fresh garlic |
| 1 | Tbsp. brown sugar |
| 1 | tsp. toasted sesame oil |
| 1/4 | tsp. red pepper flakes |
| 2 | tsp. fresh lemon juice |
| | Black pepper to taste |

**FOR THE CHICKEN, COMBINE:**

| | |
|---|---|
| 1/4 | cup all-purpose flour |
| 1/2 | tsp. *each* kosher salt and black pepper |
| 3 | eggs beaten with 1 Tbsp. water |
| 2 | cups panko |
| 2 | boneless, skinless chicken breasts (8–10 oz. *each*), halved crosswise and pounded to 1/4-inch thick |
| 4 | Tbsp. vegetable oil |

**For the sauce, simmer** broth, onions, mirin, soy sauce, ginger, garlic, brown sugar, sesame oil, and pepper flakes in a saucepan over medium-low heat until onion is soft, about 20 minutes. Stir in lemon juice and season sauce with black pepper; keep warm.

**For the chicken, combine** flour, salt, and pepper in a shallow dish. Place eggs and panko in separate shallow dishes. Coat cutlets on both sides in flour, dip into egg, then dredge in panko.

**Fry** cutlets in two batches in 2 Tbsp. oil per batch in a sauté pan over medium-high heat until browned and cooked through, about 3 minutes per side. Slice cutlets into strips; serve with sauce.

Per serving: 485 cal; 21g total fat (4g sat); 186mg chol; 1522mg sodium; 28g carb (1g fiber, 15g total sugars); 37g protein

Dredge the chicken in flour, then dip into eggs, letting excess drip off, then press into panko so it adheres.

To avoid crowding, fry cutlets two at a time, flipping as soon as they become brown and crispy.

"Crispy chicken, a super flavorful sauce, and rice to soak it all up — what more could you ask for in a quick-to-fix menu?"

**John Kirkpatrick**
Test Kitchen
Manager

# VINEGAR SUSHI RICE

*Firm, sticky Japanese-style rice is ideal for soaking up the flavorful onion sauce.*

Makes 4 servings
Total time: 30 minutes

**RINSE:**

| | |
|---|---|
| 1 | cup sushi rice |
| 1 1/4 | cups cold water |
| 1/2 | tsp. kosher salt |

**STIR IN:**

| | |
|---|---|
| 1/2 | cup sliced scallions |
| 2 | Tbsp. rice vinegar |

**Rinse** rice in cool water until water runs clear; drain. Place rice in a saucepan and stir in water and salt; bring to a boil over high heat.

**Cover** pan, reduce heat to low, and cook rice until tender and water is absorbed, about 20 minutes. Remove pan from heat and let stand, covered, 10 minutes.

**Stir in** scallions and vinegar.

Per serving: 183 cal; 0g total fat (0g sat); 0mg chol; 243mg sodium; 40g carb (2g fiber, 1g total sugars); 3g protein

# COMPOUND BUTTER

Compound butter is a mixture of butter and flavorful ingredients, such as herbs, shallots, garlic, and wine. The butter is typically rolled into a log, chilled, sliced, and served over hot steaks, or other meats or fish, to melt, releasing tons of great flavor.

**STAFF FAVORITE**

Robin loves the compound butter on this filet, giving it an extra-special kick of flavor.

## VIETNAMESE NOODLE SALAD WITH GRILLED MARINATED PORK

*The pork will have a ton of flavor after marinating for just an hour, but it's even better when it can marinate overnight.*

Makes 8 servings
Total time: 30 minutes + marinating

### FOR THE PORK, COMBINE:

| | |
|---|---|
| 1/4 | cup minced scallions |
| 2 | Tbsp. minced fresh garlic |
| 2 | Tbsp. minced fresh cilantro |
| 2 | Tbsp. *each* fish sauce and low-sodium soy sauce |
| 1 | Tbsp. sugar |
| 1 | Tbsp. toasted sesame oil |
| 1 | tsp. red pepper flakes |
| | Minced zest of 2 limes |
| 2 | lb. boneless pork shoulder roast, trimmed and thinly sliced |

### FOR THE DRESSING, HEAT:

| | |
|---|---|
| 1/2 | cup water |
| 2 | Tbsp. sugar |
| 2 | Tbsp. *each* fish sauce and rice vinegar |
| 1 | Tbsp. finely shredded carrot |
| 1 | tsp. grated fresh garlic |
| 2 | Tbsp. fresh lime juice |
| 1 | tsp. red pepper flakes |

### FOR THE SALAD, COOK:

| | |
|---|---|
| 8 | oz. medium rice-stick noodles |
| 2 | cups fresh mung bean sprouts |
| 1 | bunch fresh cilantro |
| 1 | cup fresh mint leaves |
| 1/2 | cup sliced scallions |
| 1 | English cucumber, halved lengthwise and sliced |
| 1 | cup julienned carrots |
| 1 | cup chopped dry-roasted peanuts |

**For the pork, combine** scallions, garlic, cilantro, fish sauce, soy sauce, sugar, sesame oil, pepper flakes, and zest in a bowl.

**STAFF FAVORITE** — Amanda thinks it was the combo of the marinade, the grilling, and the cut of pork that knocked this salad out of the ballpark for her.

**Add** pork to marinade, toss to coat, and marinate at least 1 hour, or up to 2 days in the refrigerator.

**For the dressing, heat** water, sugar, fish sauce, vinegar, carrot, and garlic in a saucepan over medium-high until sugar dissolves. Off heat, stir in lime juice and pepper flakes.

**For the salad, cook** noodles according to package directions; drain and rinse. Toss noodles with half the dressing.

**Preheat** grill to medium-high. Brush grill grate with oil. Grill pork, covered, until charred, 2–3 minutes per side.

**To serve, divide** noodles among eight bowls; top with pork, bean sprouts, cilantro, mint, scallions, cucumber, carrots, and peanuts. Serve salad with remaining dressing on the side.

Per serving: 466 cal; 24g total fat (6g sat); 71mg chol; 551mg sodium; 35g carb (5g fiber, 6g total sugars); 29g protein

This creamy salmon dinner can be on the table almost as fast as ordinary pasta with sauce from a jar. During the time it takes to boil water and cook farfalle, you can make the flavorful cream sauce with sautéed onions.

## SMOKED SALMON PASTA WITH CAPERS & DILL

*Be careful when seasoning this dish. The smoked salmon and capers are both salty, and you may find that you don't need any extra salt.*

Makes 4 servings
Total time: 30 minutes

**COOK:**
8    oz. farfalle pasta
**SAUTÉ:**
1    cup thinly sliced onions
1    Tbsp. olive oil
1    cup heavy cream
2    Tbsp. capers
4    oz. smoked salmon, flaked
2    Tbsp. chopped fresh dill
1    tsp. fresh lemon juice
     Salt and black pepper to taste

**Cook** farfalle in a large pot of boiling salted water according to package directions; drain.
**Sauté** onions in oil in a skillet over medium-high heat, 3 minutes. Add cream and capers; cook until liquid is reduced by half. Off heat, stir salmon, dill, lemon juice, and farfalle into cream sauce; season with salt and pepper.

Per serving: 487 cal; 27g total fat (15g sat); 74mg chol; 211mg sodium; 47g carb; (2g fiber, 5g total sugars); 15g protein

### EDITOR'S FAVORITE

Kim's family loves salmon in all its forms, so it's no surprise that this recipe tops the list of repeat perfomances at her house.

# OUR FAVORITE
# PASTAS

### SMOKED SALMON

You can use either hot- or cold-smoked salmon for this recipe. Smoking at high temperatures gives salmon the flaky texture of cooked fish, while smoking for a longer time at cooler temps gives it a softer texture, like raw fish.

# ROASTED BUTTERNUT SQUASH & WHOLE-WHEAT PENNE

*This entrée is so quick to prepare because you can easily roast the squash, boil the pasta, and cook the bacon all at once.*

Makes 4 servings
Total time: 30 minutes

| | |
|---|---|
| 1 | lb. butternut squash, peeled, seeded, cut into 1/2-inch cubes (about 2 cups) |
| 2 | Tbsp. *each* olive oil and balsamic vinegar |
| | Salt and black pepper |
| 8 | oz. dry whole-wheat penne pasta |
| 8 | oz. thick-sliced bacon, diced |
| 2 | tsp. minced fresh garlic |
| 1/2 | cup grated Parmesan |
| 2 | Tbsp. thinly sliced fresh sage |
| | Balsamic vinegar |

**Preheat** oven to 450°.

**Toss** squash with oil and vinegar, season with salt and pepper, then transfer to a baking sheet. Roast squash until tender and beginning to caramelize, about 15 minutes, stirring halfway through roasting.

**Cook** penne in a large pot of boiling salted water according to package directions; drain, reserving 1/2–1 cup pasta water.

**Cook** bacon in a sauté pan over medium heat until crisp; transfer to a paper-towel-lined plate; discard drippings. Add garlic to pan; cook 1 minute.

**Add** roasted squash, penne, and bacon to pan, tossing to combine and heat through. Add pasta water, 1/4 cup at a time, until it loosely coats the pasta.

**Off heat, toss** pasta with Parmesan and sage. Drizzle servings with balsamic vinegar.

Per serving: 659 cal; 29g total fat (10g sat); 78mg chol; 1202mg sodium; 57g carb (7g fiber, total sugars); 39g protein

Carbonara is on rotation in the Test Kitchen, but this version, developed by Robin, soon became an all-time staff favorite.

**STAFF FAVORITE**

# MEXICAN CARBONARA

*Residual heat cooks the eggs, but work quickly to prevent them from scrambling. Also, be sure to start with room temperature eggs.*

Makes 4 servings (4 cups)
Total time: 30 minutes

**COOK:**

| | |
|---|---|
| 8 | oz. spaghetti |

**WHISK:**

| | |
|---|---|
| 2 | eggs, room temperature |
| 1/2 | cup finely shredded queso fresco |
| 1/4 | cup heavy cream |
| 2 | Tbsp. adobo sauce |
| 1 | chipotle in adobo sauce, minced |

**COOK:**

| | |
|---|---|
| 4 | strips thick-sliced bacon, diced |
| 1/4 | cup diced onion |
| 2 | tsp. minced fresh garlic |

**STIR IN:**

| | |
|---|---|
| 3 | Tbsp. minced fresh cilantro Salt and black pepper to taste |

**Cook** spaghetti in a pot of boiling salted water according to package directions; reserve 1/4 cup pasta water, then drain.

**Whisk** together eggs, queso fresco, cream, adobo sauce, and chipotle.

**Cook** bacon in a sauté pan until crisp. Transfer bacon to a paper-towel-lined plate; pour off all but 2 Tbsp. drippings.

**Sweat** onion and garlic in drippings over medium-low heat until onion begins to soften, 2–3 minutes. Add spaghetti and toss to coat.

**Off heat, immediately add** egg mixture to spaghetti, while stirring quickly, until eggs cook and sauce thickens. Add reserved pasta water, as necessary, until sauce reaches desired consistency.

**Stir in** cilantro and bacon, then season pasta with salt and pepper.

Per serving: 464 cal; 21g total fat (10g sat); 139mg chol; 334mg sodium; 46g carb (3g fiber, 3g total sugars); 20g protein

When Pam brought this recipe to taste panel, we knew she had a winner. This is minimalism at its best, proving less is truly more.

## CACIO E PEPE

*The heat of the pasta melts the cheese, while a little hot, starchy pasta water emulsifies everything so the dish becomes ultra creamy.*

Makes 4 servings (6 cups)
Total time: 20 minutes

**COOK:**

12 oz. spaghetti

**MEANWHILE, HEAT:**

2 Tbsp. olive oil
2 tsp. coarsely cracked black pepper
2 Tbsp. unsalted butter

**OFF HEAT, SPRINKLE:**

1 cup grated Pecorino Romano (4 oz.), divided

**Cook** spaghetti in a large pot of boiling salted water according to package directions.

**Meanwhile, heat** oil in a sauté pan over medium until nearly shimmering; add pepper and cook until lightly toasted and fragrant, about 3 minutes. Add 1/4 cup pasta water from pasta pot. Off heat, stir in butter until melted.

**Transfer** spaghetti from pot to sauté pan using tongs, tossing with pepper mixture to coat; reserve 1 1/2 cups pasta water.

**Off heat, sprinkle** 3/4 cup Pecorino Romano into pan and toss with spaghetti until melted, adding more pasta water, 1/4 cup at a time, until it reaches a creamy consistency; serve immediately. Top servings with additional pepper and remaining 1/4 cup Pecorino Romano.

Per serving: 530 cal; 22g total fat (9g sat); 35mg chol; 561mg sodium; 62g carb; (2g fiber, 3g total sugars); 19g protein

## ORECCHIETTE ALLA NORCINA

*Orecchiette [oh-rayk-kee-EHT-teh] means "little ears" in Italian. It has a thick and chewy texture that's great with the rich and creamy sauce.*

Makes 4 servings (6 cups)
Total time: 55 minutes

**FOR THE GREMOLATA, HEAT:**

| | |
|---|---|
| 2 | Tbsp. olive oil |
| 1 | cup fresh bread crumbs |
| 1/2 | cup chopped walnuts |
| 1/2 | cup minced fresh parsley |
| 1 | Tbsp. minced lemon zest |
| | Salt to taste |

**FOR THE PASTA, COOK:**

| | |
|---|---|
| 8 | oz. orecchiette pasta |

**FOR THE SAUCE, HEAT:**

| | |
|---|---|
| 2 | Tbsp. olive oil |
| 1 | lb. boneless pork loin chops, (1/2-inch thick) trimmed, seasoned with salt and black pepper |

**ADD:**

| | |
|---|---|
| 8 | oz. cremini mushrooms, stemmed and sliced |
| 1/4 | cup minced shallots |
| 1 | Tbsp. minced fresh garlic |
| 2 | tsp. minced fresh rosemary |
| 1/2 | cup dry white wine |

**STIR IN:**

| | |
|---|---|
| 1 1/2 | cups heavy cream |
| 1/2 | cup grated Pecorino Romano |
| 1/4 | tsp. freshly grated nutmeg |
| | Salt and red pepper flakes to taste |

**For the gremolata, heat** oil in a nonstick skillet over medium. Toast bread crumbs and walnuts, 3–4 minutes; transfer to a bowl and let cool. Stir in parsley and zest and season gremolata with salt.

**For the pasta, cook** orecchiette in a pot of boiling salted water according to package directions; drain and set aside.

**STAFF FAVORITE** — This is one of Haley's favorite pasta dishes. With tender pork in a rich cream sauce, it's as comforting as it gets.

**For the sauce, heat** oil in a large skillet over medium-high until shimmering. Add pork chops; sauté until a thermometer inserted into chops registers 135°, 2 minutes per side. Transfer chops to a plate, let rest 5 minutes, then dice.

**Add** mushrooms to skillet; cook over medium-high heat until browned, 4–5 minutes. Stir in shallots, garlic, and rosemary; cook 1 minute. Deglaze skillet with wine; reduce until evaporated.

**Stir in** cream and bring sauce to a boil. Reduce heat to medium and simmer sauce until thickened, 5–6 minutes.

**Stir in** Pecorino Romano, nutmeg, orecchiette, and pork to heat through; season with salt and pepper flakes. Top servings with gremolata.

Per serving: 1016 cal; 65g total fat (27g sat); 187mg chol; 426mg sodium; 61g carb; (5g fiber, 8g total sugars); 43g protein

# RAMEN NOODLES & MEATBALLS

*If you like spaghetti and meatballs, and you like pot stickers, this dish is the best of both worlds — long pasta with Asian-flavored meatballs and sauce.*

Makes 6 servings
Total time: about 1 hour

**FOR THE MEATBALLS, COMBINE:**

1    egg
1/2  cup panko
2    scallions, minced
2    Tbsp. minced fresh ginger
1    Tbsp. *each* low-sodium soy
     sauce and mirin *or* dry sherry
1    tsp. kosher salt
1/2  tsp. sugar
1    lb. ground pork
2    ice cubes

**FOR THE SAUCE, SEAR:**

2    Tbsp. sesame oil

**ADD:**

1    bunch scallion whites,
     minced (greens reserved)
2    Tbsp. *each* grated fresh
     garlic and ginger
2    cans diced tomatoes
     (14.5 oz. each), drained
2    cups low-sodium beef stock
1/4  cup low-sodium soy sauce
1    Tbsp. mirin
2    tsp. chili garlic sauce

**COVER:**

3    pkg. ramen noodles (3 oz.
     *each*), seasoning packets
     discarded
     Boiling water
     Sliced scallion greens

**For the meatballs, combine** egg, panko, scallions, ginger, soy sauce, mirin, salt, and sugar in the bowl of a stand mixer; add pork and ice.
**Cover** bowl of mixer with plastic wrap and beat pork mixture with the paddle attachment on medium speed until mixture starts coming together and looks pasty, 1 minute; discard ice cubes. Scoop meatballs with a #30 scoop (2 Tbsp.) onto a baking sheet; chill while preparing ingredients for the sauce.
**For the sauce, sear** meatballs in oil in a large sauté pan over high heat until brown on all sides, 5–6 minutes; transfer to a plate. Reduce heat to medium.
**Add** scallion whites, garlic, and grated ginger, and cook, stirring constantly, 30 seconds. Add tomatoes, stock, soy sauce, mirin, and chili garlic sauce. Add meatballs and any residual juices on plate; simmer, covered, until meatballs are cooked through, about 12 minutes. Transfer meatballs to a serving dish; cover to keep warm.
**Cover** noodles with boiling water and soak, covered, 2 minutes; drain. Toss ramen noodles with sauce and serve with meatballs; top with scallion greens.

Per serving: 493 cal; 22g total fat (7g sat); 85mg chol; 1366mg sodium; 49g carb (5g fiber, 7g total sugars); 24g protein

"I love spaghetti and meatballs, but I'd never had them like this before. This Asian-style dish resulted in an instant classic dubbed ramghetti & meatballs."

Maddy Bendgen
Assistant Editor

## ONE-POT RAGU WITH ITALIAN SAUSAGE

Makes 5 servings (about 9 cups)
Total time: 30 minutes

**MINCE:**

| | |
|---|---|
| 1/2 | cup *each* chopped carrot, celery, and onion |
| 3 | cloves garlic |

**HEAT:**

| | |
|---|---|
| 2 | Tbsp. olive oil |
| 1 | lb. bulk Italian sausage |

**STIR IN:**

| | |
|---|---|
| 1 | can petite diced tomatoes (28 oz.) |
| 3 | cups low-sodium chicken broth |
| 1 | Tbsp. dried Italian seasoning |
| 8 | oz. spaghetti, broken in half |
| | Salt and black pepper to taste |
| 1/2 | cup chopped fresh basil |

**Mince** carrot, celery, onion and garlic in a food processor.

**Heat** oil in a large saucepan over medium-high. Add sausage and minced vegetables; sauté until meat is browned, 5 minutes.

**Stir in** tomatoes, broth, Italian seasoning, and spaghetti. Make sure noodles are submerged in liquid; bring to a boil. Cover, reduce heat to medium-low, and cook until pasta is al dente and sauce has thickened, 8–10 minutes. Season ragu with salt and pepper.

**Stir in** basil before serving.

Per serving: 406 cal; 19g total fat (4g sat); 55mg chol; 728mg sodium; 36g carb (2g fiber, 7g total sugars); 18g protein

**FAN FAVORITE**

When you pair ragu and pasta, it's easy to see why this classic dish is truly a favorite.

# WARM & HEARTY
# BAKED
# PASTAS

Who says LASAGNA requires tomato sauce? The garlic–herb cheese creates a sauce that's similar to rich Alfredo. Assemble towering layers of chicken, mushrooms, and spinach, and you'll have one impressive lasagna.

## BOURSIN CHICKEN LASAGNA

*It's important to press down each layer as it's completed — eight unpressed layers would tower over the top of the baking dish.*

Makes 12 servings
Total time: 2 hours

### SAUTÉ:

| | |
|---|---|
| 2 | cups sliced leeks |
| 2 | Tbsp. olive oil |
| 1 | lb. sliced button mushrooms |
| 1/2 | tsp. red pepper flakes |
| 1/3 | cup all-purpose flour |

### DEGLAZE:

| | |
|---|---|
| 1/2 | cup dry sherry |
| 3 | cups whole *or* 2% milk |
| 1/2 | cup low-sodium chicken broth |
| 2 | Tbsp. fresh lemon juice |

### WHISK IN:

| | |
|---|---|
| 2 | pkg. Garlic and Fine Herbs Boursin cheese (5 oz. *each*), crumbled |
| 1 | box frozen chopped spinach (10 oz.), thawed and squeezed dry |

### ARRANGE:

| | |
|---|---|
| 24 | sheets no-boil lasagna (about two 8 oz. pkg.) |
| 4 | cups shredded *or* chopped cooked chicken *or* turkey |
| 1 1/2 | lb. fresh mozzarella, sliced into 42 rounds |
| 1 | cup shredded Parmesan |

**Preheat** oven to 400°. Coat a 9×13-inch baking dish with nonstick spray.

**Sauté** leeks in oil in a saucepan over medium-high heat for the sauce. Add mushrooms and pepper flakes; cook until mushrooms are soft, 3 minutes. Stir in flour to coat and cook 2 minutes.

**Deglaze** pan with sherry; reduce until nearly absorbed. Gradually add milk, broth, and lemon juice, stirring until smooth. Simmer sauce until thickened, about 5 minutes.

**Whisk in** Boursin in batches until smooth. Stir in spinach. Reserve 1 cup sauce for top of lasagna. Spread 1/3 cup sauce on bottom of prepared baking dish.

**Arrange** three pasta sheets across bottom of baking dish, then spread about 1 cup sauce over them. Scatter about 1/2 cup chicken on sauce, top with 6 mozzarella slices, and sprinkle with 2 Tbsp. Parmesan. Repeat layers with remaining pasta, sauce, chicken, mozzarella, and Parmesan. Top last layer with reserved sauce and sprinkle with remaining 2 Tbsp. Parmesan.

**Bake** lasagna, uncovered, until bubbly and brown, 30–35 minutes; let rest 20–30 minutes to set before cutting and serving.

Per serving: 625 cal; 33g total fat (18g sat); 130mg chol; 426mg sodium; 40g carb (2g fiber, 5g total sugars); 39g protein

### STEPS TO LASAGNA SUCCESS

Stir in flour — it will thicken the sauce once the milk and broth are added, and it will give the sauce body.

Use three sheets of lasagna for each of the eight layers, including sauce, chicken, and cheese in between.

**STAFF FAVORITE**

With eight layers of chicken, an abundance of earthy mushrooms, and a garlic-herb triple cream cheese sauce, this is one lasagna recipe we make for special occasions.

# CASSEROLE
# COMFORT

Nothing says comfort better than a piping hot pasta coming straight out of the oven. From a sophisticated crab casserole, to cheesy stuffed shells, our favorite lasagna recipe, to a tweak on an Italian classic, this section of BAKED PASTA DISHES is certain to strike a culinary chord.

## CRAB MAC 'N CHEESE

Makes 8 servings
Total time: 1 hour

| | |
|---|---|
| 1 | cup fresh bread crumbs |
| 1 | cup grated Parmesan, divided |
| 1/3 | cup chopped fresh parsley |
| 2 | Tbsp. unsalted butter, melted |
| | Salt and black pepper to taste |
| 8 | oz. cavatappi pasta |
| 2 | Tbsp. unsalted butter |
| 3 | Tbsp. minced shallots |
| 1 | Tbsp. minced fresh garlic |
| 3 | Tbsp. all-purpose flour |
| 2³/4 | cups half-and-half, warmed |
| 1 | tsp. Old Bay seasoning |
| 1/4 | tsp. freshly grated nutmeg |
| 8 | oz. fontina cheese, shredded |
| 8 | oz. premium *or* pasteurized lump crabmeat, drained |
| | Cayenne pepper to taste |

**Preheat** oven to 400°. Coat a 1¹/2-quart baking dish with nonstick spray.

**Combine** bread crumbs, ¹/2 cup Parmesan, parsley, and melted butter for the topping; season with salt and black pepper.

**Cook** cavatappi in a pot of boiling salted water according to package directions; drain.

**Melt** 2 Tbsp. butter in a saucepan over medium heat. Add shallots and garlic; sweat 5 minutes. Increase heat to medium-high. Whisk in flour; cook 1 minute.

**Whisk in** half-and-half, Old Bay, and nutmeg until smooth; bring to a boil, then reduce heat and simmer, whisking often, until thickened about 2 minutes. Reduce heat to low.

**Add** fontina and remaining ¹/2 cup Parmesan by the handful, whisking after each addition until melted.

**Off heat, stir in** crab, season with salt, black pepper, and cayenne, then stir in cavatappi. Transfer mac 'n cheese to prepared dish; sprinkle on topping.

**Bake** mac 'n cheese until bubbly, and topping is golden brown, about 15 minutes; let rest 5 minutes before serving.

Per serving: 492 cal; 29g total fat (18g sat); 115mg chol; 597mg sodium; 31g carb (1g fiber, 6g total sugars); 24g protein

## SPINACH & THREE CHEESE STUFFED SHELLS

Makes 4 servings (20 shells)
Total time: 45 minutes

| | |
|---|---|
| 20 | conchiglioni |
| 1 | pkg. fresh spinach (5 oz.) |
| 2 | tsp. olive oil |
| 1 | tsp. minced fresh garlic |
| 1 | can tomato purée (10 oz.) |
| 1¹/₂ | cups whole-milk ricotta cheese |
| 1 | cup shredded mozzarella |
| 1 | cup shredded Parmesan |
| 1 | Tbsp. minced lemon zest |
| ¹/₂ | tsp. freshly grated nutmeg |
| | Salt, black pepper, and red pepper flakes to taste |
| 1 | cup cherry tomatoes |
| | Shredded Parmesan |
| | Chopped fresh parsley |

**Preheat** oven to 400°. Coat a shallow 9×13-inch gratin dish (or individual dishes) with nonstick spray.

**Cook** shells in a pot of boiling salted water just until pliable, 8–9 minutes. Drain shells over spinach in a colander, then transfer shells to a bowl and rinse with cold water; drain. Drain spinach, squeeze dry with paper towels, and chop.

**Heat** oil in a saucepan over medium. Stir in garlic; cook 1 minute. Add tomato purée; cook to heat through, 2–3 minutes. Cover bottom of prepared dish with sauce.

**Combine** ricotta, mozzarella, 1 cup Parmesan, spinach, zest, and nutmeg; season with salt, black pepper, and pepper flakes. Stuff shells and arrange in dish, cheese sides up. Scatter cherry tomatoes and more shredded Parmesan over shells. Bake shells until beginning to brown, 25–30 minutes. Sprinkle parsley over shells and serve.

Per serving: 557 cal; 27g total fat (15g sat); 77mg chol; 615mg sodium; 45g carb; (5g fiber, 7g total sugars); 33g protein

IT WOULDN'T BE UNUSUAL FOR A COUPLE OF SHELLS TO FALL APART WHILE COOKING, OR TEAR WHILE BEING STUFFED. SO, JUST IN CASE, COOK A FEW EXTRA SHELLS.

# CRAZY FOR
# CAVATELLI

# BOLOGNESE CAVATELLI WITH MEATBALLS

*Bake the meatballs separately on a preheated baking sheet before combining with pasta mixture to speed up the cooking process and help render the fat.*

Makes 10 servings (about 30 meatballs)
Total time: 1½ hours

**FOR THE SAUCE & PASTA, COOK:**

1    lb. cavatelli pasta

**MINCE:**

1    cup *each* chopped onions, carrots, and celery

4    cloves garlic

2    Tbsp. olive oil

**ADD:**

1    Tbsp. tomato paste

2    tsp. dried Italian seasoning

1    tsp. *each* kosher salt and black pepper

½    tsp. red pepper flakes

2    dried bay leaves

**STIR IN:**

1    can diced tomatoes in juice (28 oz.)

1    can crushed tomatoes (28 oz.)

1    cup low-sodium chicken broth

½    cup dry red wine

½    cup grated Romano (2 oz.)
     Pinch of sugar

**FOR THE MEATBALLS, COMBINE:**

8    oz. *each* ground pork and ground sirloin

½    cup grated onion

¼    cup dried bread crumbs

¼    cup minced fresh parsley

1    egg

2    Tbsp. minced fresh garlic

1    Tbsp. fennel seeds

1    tsp. *each* dried Italian seasoning and kosher salt

½    tsp. black pepper

8    oz. shredded part-skim mozzarella

**Preheat** oven to 400° with a parchment-lined baking sheet inside. Coat a 9×13-inch baking dish with nonstick spray.

**For the sauce and pasta, cook** cavatelli in a large pot of boiling salted water until slightly underdone, 6–7 minutes; drain.

**Mince** onions, carrots, celery, and garlic in a food processor. Sweat onion mixture in oil in a sauté pan over medium heat until liquid evaporates, 8–10 minutes.

**Add** tomato paste; cook 1 minute. Stir in Italian seasoning, salt, black pepper, pepper flakes, and bay leaves.

**Stir in** diced and crushed tomatoes, broth, wine, Romano, and sugar. Simmer sauce over medium-high heat, stirring often, until thick and bubbly, about 30 minutes. Remove bay leaves and stir in cavatelli.

**For the meatballs, combine** pork, sirloin, onion, bread crumbs, parsley, egg, garlic, fennel seeds, Italian seasoning, salt, and black pepper in a bowl. Measure meatballs using a #30 scoop (about 2 Tbsp.), place on preheated baking sheet, form into rounds, and bake 15 minutes.

**Arrange** meatballs in bottom of prepared baking dish; top with pasta mixture and mozzarella.

**Cover** casserole with foil and bake 15 minutes; uncover and bake 15 minutes more. Let casserole rest 10 minutes before serving.

Per serving: 477 cal; 17g total fat (7g sat); 65mg chol; 1097mg sodium; 52g carb (3g fiber, 9g total sugars); 26g protein

## STEPS TO CAVATELLI SUCCESS

So the sauce is smooth instead of chunky, mince the vegetables and garlic in a food processor.

To prevent liquid from splattering without trapping in moisture, cover the saucepan with a splash guard.

Measure out meatballs using a #30 scoop, place on preheated baking sheet, and form into rounds.

This is the absolute best chocolate chip cookie recipe ever. Two types of chocolate, a combo of butter and shortening, and an easy mixing method give these cookies a soft texture and delicious taste that's sure to be noticed.

## CHOCOLATE CHIP COOKIES

*A cookie scoop not only makes it easy to portion the dough, it also packs it into the scoop, producing thick, uniform cookies.*

Makes 3 dozen cookies
Total time: 30 minutes + chilling

**WHISK:**
3 1/4   cups all-purpose flour
1     tsp. *each* baking soda and table salt

**CREAM:**
1     cup *each* granulated sugar and packed dark brown sugar
2/3   cup unsalted butter, softened
2/3   cup shortening
2     eggs
2     tsp. pure vanilla extract
2     cups semisweet chocolate chips
1/2   cup milk chocolate chips

**Preheat** oven to 350°. Line 2 baking sheets with parchment paper.
**Whisk** together flour, baking soda, and salt in a bowl.

**Cream** granulated sugar, brown sugar, butter, shortening, eggs, and vanilla in a large bowl with a hand mixer on low speed. Increase speed to high and beat until mixture is fluffy and lighter in color.
**Stir** flour mixture into creamed mixture until no flour is visible. Stir in chocolate chips, cover, and chill at least 1 hour.
**Form** cookies using a #30 scoop (2 Tbsp.). Drop dough onto prepared baking sheets 2 inches apart.
**Bake** cookies on center rack until lightly brown around the edges, 12–14 minutes. Let cookies sit on baking sheet 2 minutes to set up, then transfer to a wire rack to cool.

Per cookie: 214 cal; 11g total fat (6g sat); 21mg chol; 106mg sodium; 28g carb (0g fiber, 19g total sugars); 2g protein

**STAFF**
**FAVORITE**
Robin loves to bake cookies, and once she tried this recipe, she knew she'd struck gold and has never looked back.

# OUR FAVORITE
# DESSERTS

ALL-TIME **FAVORITES**

# BEST-EVER
# CAKE

**FAN FAVORITE**

OLD-FASHIONED CHOCOLATE CAKE is not only a favorite on our website, but the staff makes this recipe in their own home kitchens for celebrations. It's the kind of cake grandma used to make, with "Betty Crocker" looks and one-of-a-kind flavor. Not only is the cake super moist, it's almost as easy to prepare as a box mix. And the thick layer of smooth icing really seals the deal.

# CHOCOLATE CAKE

*Besides making two 8-inch rounds, this recipe also makes one 9x13-inch cake (bake 35–40 minutes) or 24 cupcakes (bake 20–25 minutes). Cooled cakes may be frozen — thaw slightly before frosting.*

Makes 12 servings
Total Time: 45 minutes + cooling

**SIFT:**

3    cups all-purpose flour
2    cups sugar
1/2  cup unsweetened cocoa powder
2    tsp. baking soda
1    tsp. table salt

**COMBINE:**

2    cups hot water
3/4  cup vegetable oil
2    Tbsp. distilled white vinegar
1    Tbsp. instant espresso powder
1    Tbsp. pure vanilla extract

**Preheat** oven to 350° with rack in the center. Coat two 8-inch-round cake pans with nonstick spray.
**Sift** together flour, sugar, cocoa powder, baking soda, and salt.
**Combine** water, oil, vinegar, espresso powder, and vanilla in a large measuring cup. Add to the dry ingredients and whisk just until combined — a few lumps are okay.
**Divide** batter among prepared pans (about 3 cups in each), then bake until a toothpick inserted in centers comes out clean, 35–40 minutes. Cool cakes 15 minutes on a rack, then run a knife around edges to loosen cakes, and turn out onto the rack. Leave cakes upside down to cool completely (this flattens domed cakes), then frost.

Per serving: 688 cal; 41g total fat (19g sat); 72mg chol; 423mg sodium; 84g carb (2g fiber, 53g total sugars); 7g protein

Combine wet ingredients with dry, whisking just to combine. Do not overmix or cake could be tough.

For the icing, add cream mixture to chocolate mixture and cook, whisking, until smooth.

When a toothpick inserted into centers of cakes comes out clean, they're done. Cool cakes completely.

Spread 1 cup icing all the way to the edges of first layer.

# GLOSSY CHOCOLATE ICING

*If the icing seems too soft, chill it briefly to help it set up.*

Makes about 4 cups
Total Time: 10 Minutes + cooling

**MELT:**

1    stick unsalted butter (8 Tbsp.)

**STIR IN:**

1 1/2  cups sugar
1 1/4  cups unsweetened cocoa powder, sifted
       Pinch of table salt

**WHISK:**

1 1/4  cups heavy cream
1/4    cup sour cream
1      tsp. instant espresso powder

**OFF HEAT, STIR IN:**

2    tsp. pure vanilla extract

**Melt** butter in a large saucepan over medium heat.
**Stir in** sugar, cocoa powder, and salt. Mixture will be thick and grainy.
**Whisk** together heavy cream, sour cream, and espresso powder in a large measuring cup until smooth. Gradually whisk cream mixture into butter mixture until blended and smooth. Cook mixture until sugar dissolves and icing is smooth and hot to the touch. Do not boil.
**Off heat, stir in** vanilla. Cool icing at room temperature until spreadable, about 3 hours.

# FRENCH APPLE-CUSTARD PIE

*Pink Lady or Honeycrisp apples are the best choice for this pie. They're crisp, crunchy, sweet, and tart — and available year-round.*

Makes 8 servings
Total time: about 1¼ hours + chilling

**FOR THE CRUST, PREPARE:**

- 1 recipe Best-Ever Pie Crust (cuisineathome.com) *or* purchased pie dough

**FOR THE FILLING, MELT:**

- 2 Tbsp. unsalted butter
- 2 lb. apples, such as Pink Lady *or* Honeycrisp, peeled, cored, and thinly sliced (4–6 total)
- 2 Tbsp. sugar
- 1 Tbsp. dark rum *or* apple cider
- ¼ tsp. table salt, divided
- 2 eggs
- 2 egg yolks
- 1 cup heavy cream
- ½ cup sugar
- 1 tsp. pure vanilla extract
- ⅛ tsp. freshly grated nutmeg

**FOR THE TOPPING, COMBINE:**

- 1 cup sliced almonds
- ⅓ cup sugar
- 2 Tbsp. unsalted butter, softened
  Pinch of table salt

ONLINE EXTRA
Best-Ever Pie Crust
CuisineAtHome.com

**Preheat** oven to 400° with rack in bottom position.

**For the crust, prepare** pie crust (for a 9-inch pie plate) according to recipe and rolling directions. Prick dough with a fork and chill 15 minutes. Line the pie shell with foil and fill with dried beans or rice. Blind bake shell until set but not browned, 18–20 minutes; remove foil and beans. Bake crust until pale golden, 5 minutes; cool completely.

**Reduce** oven temperature to 325°.

**For the filling, melt** 2 Tbsp. butter in a sauté pan over medium heat. Add apples and 2 Tbsp. sugar; sauté until apples are soft but not mushy, 8–10 minutes. Stir in rum and ⅛ tsp. salt. Spread apples over bottom of blind-baked pie crust.

**Whisk** together eggs, egg yolks, cream, ½ cup sugar, vanilla, nutmeg, and remaining ⅛ tsp. salt; pour over apples in pie crust. Bake pie until custard is barely set in center, about 30 minutes.

**For the topping, combine** almonds, sugar, and butter. Remove pie from oven; sprinkle with topping. Cover pie with a pie shield if edge of crust seems to be overbrowning.

**Return** pie to oven; bake until custard is almost set but still slightly jiggly in center, 15–20 minutes more. Let pie cool completely, then chill; bring to room temperature before serving.

Per serving: 560 cal; 36g total fat (18g sat); 164mg chol; 127mg sodium; 55g carb (5g fiber, 34g total sugars); 8g protein

To core an apple, stand it on its blossom end and slice off the four lobes around the core.

Just a touch of rum adds a delicious flavor to the sautéed apples. Apple cider can be substituted.

Thoroughly whisk together the egg mixture before pouring it over the apples in the crust.

ONLINE FAVORITE

The analytics don't lie — this pie has been searched for more than any other pie in the 22 years of publishing Cuisine at Home magazine, and that's saying something.

## MAKE IT AHEAD

This pie absolutely must be made ahead, and a day ahead is best. The custard needs time to cool and set completely before it can be sliced. Chill the pie in the refrigerator overnight, then bring it to room temperature before serving.

## SKINNING HAZELNUTS

The skins of hazelnuts can be bitter. To remove them, boil 2 cups water plus 3 Tbsp. baking soda, and add the nuts. After 3–5 minutes, shock the nuts in ice water — the skins will rub right off. Be sure to dry the nuts well before toasting them.

## NECTARINE TORTE WITH HAZELNUTS & ORANGE

*Tortes are rich cakes often made with little or no flour, but usually include ground nuts or bread crumbs.*

Makes 12 servings (³/₄ cup sauce)
Total time: 30 minutes + baking

### FOR THE TORTE, PROCESS:

- ³/₄  cup granulated sugar
- ¹/₂  cup skinned and toasted hazelnuts (2.5 oz.)

### ADD:

- ³/₄  cup all-purpose flour
- ¹/₂  tsp. baking powder
- ¹/₄  tsp. table salt
- 6  Tbsp. unsalted butter, cubed
- 2  eggs
- 1  tsp. pure vanilla extract
   Minced zest of 1 orange
- 1  lb. ripe, slightly firm nectarines, cut into eighths

### FOR THE SAUCE, COOK:

- ¹/₂  cup orange marmalade
- ¹/₄  cup brandy
- 2  Tbsp. light brown sugar
   Juice of 1 orange
   Powdered sugar

**Preheat** oven to 350°. Coat a 9-inch springform pan with nonstick spray and flour.

**For the torte, process** sugar and hazelnuts in a food processor until nuts are finely ground, 1 minute. **Add** flour, baking powder, and salt; pulse to combine. Add butter and pulse until mixture resembles coarse sand, about 10 seconds. Add eggs, vanilla, and zest, and process until smooth, 10 seconds.

**Transfer** batter to prepared pan; spread batter evenly and smooth surface. Arrange nectarines, skin sides up, over surface of batter.

**Bake** torte until golden brown and a toothpick inserted into the center comes out with few crumbs, 40–45 minutes.

**Run** a knife around edges to loosen torte; let cool in pan on a rack to room temperature, about 30 minutes.

**For the sauce, cook** marmalade, brandy, brown sugar, and orange juice in a small saucepan over medium-high heat until thick and syrupy, 10 minutes.

**Remove** cooled torte from pan, dust with powdered sugar, and serve with sauce.

Per serving: 244 cal; 10g total fat (4g sat); 46mg chol; 83mg sodium; 35g carb (1g fiber, 27g total sugars); 3g protein

To keep the nuts from turning into a butter-like consistency, pulse them with the sugar until finely ground.

The batter is thick, so use an offset spatula to smooth and evenly spread it to the edges of the pan.

STAFF
FAVORITE

Like the filling of a fine chocolate
truffle, this luscious cheesecake
is Amanda's favorite.

What you get when you combine two favorite sweets — CHEESECAKE AND CHOCOLATE — into one indulgent dessert is a wonderfully rich eating experience that no one can resist.

## CHOCOLATE TRUFFLE CHEESECAKE

*For the best flavor and texture, remove the cheesecake from the refrigerator 30 minutes before you plan to serve it.*

Makes 16 servings
Total time: 2 hours + chilling

**FOR THE CRUST, PROCESS:**

2   sleeves chocolate graham crackers, 18 crackers (2$\frac{1}{4}$ cups crumbs)
1   Tbsp. sugar
    Pinch of table salt
1   stick unsalted butter (8 Tbsp.), melted

**FOR THE CHEESECAKE, MELT:**

12  oz. bittersweet bar chocolate, chopped
2   Tbsp. unsalted butter
2   tsp. instant espresso powder

**BEAT:**

1   lb. cream cheese, softened
1   cup sugar
3   eggs
1   cup heavy cream, whipped
2   tsp. pure vanilla extract

**FOR THE GANACHE, HEAT:**

$\frac{1}{2}$  cup heavy cream
4   oz. semisweet chocolate chips ($\frac{3}{4}$ cup)

**Preheat** oven to 325°.

**For the crust, process** graham crackers, sugar, and salt in a food processor until fine. Drizzle in melted butter and process until combined. Press crumbs into bottom and up sides of a 9-inch springform pan. Bake crust 10 minutes; set aside.

**For the cheesecake, melt** chocolate with butter and espresso powder in a double boiler; set aside to cool slightly.

**Beat** cream cheese and sugar in a stand mixer or a large bowl with a hand mixer until smooth, scraping sides of bowl as needed. Add eggs, one at a time, mixing well after each addition. Add melted chocolate mixture to batter and beat until combined.

**Fold** whipped cream and vanilla into batter, then pour into crust; bake until edges are set but center is still jiggly, 40–45 minutes.

**Turn** oven off; leave cheesecake in oven with door closed, 30 minutes.

**Remove** cheesecake from oven; cool completely, then cover and chill at least 4 hours, or overnight.

**For the ganache, heat** cream in a microwave in a heatproof bowl on high until boiling, 1–2 minutes. Add chocolate chips and let sit 2 minutes, then stir until smooth. Cool ganache, 5 minutes. Drizzle cheesecake with ganache, then top with fresh raspberries and chocolate curls, if desired.

**To cut cheesecake,** remove sides from the pan, then slice with a sharp knife dipped in hot water and wiped dry before each slice.

Per serving: 462 cal; 36g total fat (21g sat); 108mg chol; 152mg sodium; 36g carb (0g fiber, 31g total sugars); 6g protein

Press crust mixture on the bottom and up the sides of a springform pan with the back of a spoon.

To avoid deflating whipped cream, gently fold it in with a spatula just until there are no streaks.

"Seven layers of pure heaven"
is what John calls these bars,
and "they're so easy to make."

# CHOCOLATE-CRUSTED SEVEN-LAYER BARS

*For peanut bars, use all graham crackers for the crust. Substitute milk chocolate chips for the semisweet chips, peanut butter chips for the butterscotch chips, and chopped dry-roasted peanuts for the almonds.*

Makes 32 bars
Total time: 20 minutes + baking and cooling

**MELT:**

| | |
|---|---|
| 2 | sticks unsalted butter (16 Tbsp.) |
| 2 | Tbsp. sugar |
| 1/4 | tsp. table salt |
| 1 | pkg. Nabisco's Famous chocolate wafers (9 oz.) *or* 9 oz. chocolate graham crackers (18 crackers) |
| 9 | regular graham crackers (4.5 oz.) |

**LAYER:**

| | |
|---|---|
| 1 | cup *each* semisweet chocolate chips and butterscotch chips |
| 1 1/2 | cups sweetened shredded coconut |
| 1 | cup sliced almonds |
| 1 | can sweetened condensed milk (14 oz.) |

**Preheat** oven to 350°. Coat a 9×13-inch baking pan with nonstick spray. Line bottom of pan with parchment paper, then coat paper with nonstick spray.
**Melt** butter in a large saucepan over low heat for the crust, 2 minutes. Add sugar and salt and stir to dissolve; remove from heat.
**Process** chocolate wafers in a food processor to fine crumbs; transfer to a bowl. Process graham crackers to fine crumbs; stir into chocolate wafer crumbs.
**Pour** crumb mixture into butter mixture; stir to thoroughly combine. Press crumb crust into bottom of prepared pan.
**Layer** crust with chocolate chips, butterscotch chips, coconut, and almonds, spreading ingredients evenly. Pour sweetened condensed milk over the top layer.

**Bake** bars until nuts and coconut are lightly toasted, 35–40 minutes; remove from oven. Let bars cool in pan on a rack, 45 minutes, then refrigerate at least 2 hours.
**Place** cutting board over pan and invert. Tap bottom of pan to release crust; peel off parchment paper and cut into 32 bars.

Per bar: 93 cal; 18g total fat (11g sat); 19mg chol; 144mg sodium; 32g carb (2g fiber, 23g total sugars); 4g protein

Combine the processed chocolate wafers and graham crackers; add to the butter mixture and stir well.

Press the crust mixture into the pan, leveling it out all the way to the ends and to the sides.

Pour the sweetened condensed milk over the top layer, drizzling the milk from side to side.

Flip the bars out of the pan so that the crust is on top. Use a large chef's knife to cut the bars evenly.

# WE'RE SWEET ON
# STRAWBERRY SHORTCAKE

## MAKE IT AHEAD

Make-ahead components streamline this party-perfect dessert.
The biscuits hold up well (and can even be frozen), the strawberries
taste great after standing for several hours or even overnight,
and it's fine to make the sauce beforehand and rewarm it.

# CHOCOLATE-COVERED STRAWBERRY SHORTCAKES

*Frozen strawberries in syrup are usually too mushy to be eaten straight from the package, but they make a flavorful base for fresh strawberries.*

Makes 6 servings
Total time: 1½ hours

**FOR THE SHORTCAKES, WHISK:**

1¾    cups all-purpose flour
3    Tbsp. granulated sugar
1    Tbsp. baking powder
½    tsp. table salt

**CUT:**

4    Tbsp. cold unsalted butter, cubed
¼    cup chopped semisweet bar chocolate
½    cup heavy cream
⅓    cup plain yogurt

**BRUSH:**

   Heavy cream
   Sparkling *or* granulated sugar

**FOR THE STRAWBERRIES, CRUSH:**

1    box frozen strawberries in syrup (10 oz.), thawed
4    cups fresh strawberries, hulled and halved
¼    cup granulated sugar
2    tsp. fresh lemon juice

**FOR THE WHIPPED CREAM, BEAT:**

½    cup heavy cream
2    Tbsp. powdered sugar
½    tsp. pure vanilla extract

**FOR THE CHOCOLATE SAUCE, HEAT:**

⅓    cup heavy cream
1    Tbsp. light corn syrup
4    oz. semisweet bar chocolate, chopped

**Preheat** oven to 425°. Line a baking sheet with parchment.

**For the shortcakes, whisk** together flour, granulated sugar, baking powder, and salt.

**Cut** butter into flour mixture using a pastry blender until butter is pea-sized; stir in chocolate.

**Stir** together cream and yogurt in a separate bowl, then add to flour mixture, blending with a fork just until dough comes together.

**Pat out** dough on a lightly floured surface into a 1-inch-thick circle. Using a 2½-inch-round cutter, cut out as many shortcakes as possible and place on prepared baking sheet. Gently press scraps back together and cut remaining shortcakes to make six total.

**Brush** tops of shortcakes with cream and sprinkle with sparkling sugar. Bake shortcakes until golden, about 15 minutes.

**For the strawberries, crush** thawed strawberries in a bowl with a potato masher. Stir in fresh strawberries, sugar, and lemon juice. Let fruit mixture stand at least 30 minutes, or overnight in the refrigerator.

**For the whipped cream, beat** cream, powdered sugar, and vanilla with a hand mixer until soft peaks form.

**For the chocolate sauce, heat** cream and corn syrup in a small saucepan over medium until simmering. Place chocolate in a bowl and pour cream mixture over; let stand about 5 minutes, then whisk until smooth.

**To assemble, split** shortcakes; coat cut sides with strawberry juices. Place bottoms on serving dishes, then top with strawberries, whipped cream, chocolate sauce, and remaining shortcake halves.

Per serving: 647 cal; 37g total fat (23g sat); 81mg chol; 497mg sodium; 80g carb (4g fiber, 46g total sugars; 8g protein

## STEPS TO SHORTCAKE SUCCESS

It's easiest to cut butter into dry ingredients using a pastry blender, but you can also use two knives.

To prevent sticking, dust the cutter with flour before cutting each cake. Take care not to twist the cutter.

Coarse-grain sparkling sugar gives the shortcakes loads of crunchy texture, but any type of sugar will do.

# STRAWBERRY SHORTCAKE BARS WITH FRESH STRAWBERRY TOPPING

*If you love strawberry shortcake, these bars are for you. With incredible fresh strawberry flavor in every bite, there's no holding back.*

Makes 12 servings
Total time: 1¼ hours + cooling

**FOR THE BARS, WHISK:**
- 2 cups all-purpose flour
- ¼ cup granulated sugar
- 1 Tbsp. baking powder
- ½ tsp. table salt

**CUT:**
- 1 stick cold unsalted butter (8 Tbsp.), cubed
- 1 cup diced fresh strawberries
- 4 oz. white bar chocolate, chopped
- ½ cup heavy cream
- 1 egg
- ½ tsp. pure vanilla extract
- ¾ cup strawberry jam
  Sparkling sugar, *optional*

**FOR THE TOPPING, PURÉE:**
- 4 cups fresh strawberries, hulled, halved *or* quartered if large, and divided
- ⅓ cup granulated sugar
- 1 Tbsp. cornstarch
- ¼ cup water
  Pinch of table salt
- 1–2 drops red food color, *optional*
  Whipped cream

**Preheat** oven to 375°. Coat a 9-inch-square baking pan with nonstick spray. Line pan with a 2-inch overhang of parchment paper; coat with nonstick spray.

**For the bars, whisk** together flour, granulated sugar, baking powder, and salt in a bowl.

**Cut** butter into flour mixture using a pastry blender until butter is pea-sized; stir in strawberries and white chocolate.

**Whisk** together heavy cream, egg, and vanilla, then add to flour mixture, blending with a fork just until dough comes together.

**Press** half the dough onto bottom of prepared pan. Spread jam over dough, then pat remaining dough over the top; sprinkle with sparkling sugar. Bake bars until lightly golden, 35–40 minutes; cool to room temperature, then cut into 12 bars.

**For the topping, purée** ¾ cup halved or quartered strawberries in a food processor. Combine sugar and cornstarch in a saucepan. Stir in puréed strawberries, water, and pinch of salt; bring to a boil and cook until thick, stirring constantly, about 3 minutes. Stir in food color, then remove from heat and let cool slightly; pour over remaining 3¼ cups strawberries. Let topping cool to room temperature, or refrigerate until ready to serve.

**Serve** bars with topping and whipped cream.

Per serving: 342 cal; 16g total fat (10g sat); 51mg chol; 253mg sodium; 49g carb (2g fiber, 29g total sugars); 4g protein

**STAFF FAVORITE**

Whenever Maddy takes these bars to a gathering, she makes sure to bring a copy of the recipe, because it never fails — someone always asks for one.

# STRAWBERRY-CHOCOLATE SHORTCAKE COOKIES

Makes 36 (3-inch) cookies
Total time: 1¹/₂ hours + chilling

| | |
|---|---|
| 10 | oz. fresh strawberries |
| 2 | sticks unsalted butter (16 Tbsp.), softened |
| 1¹/₂ | cups granulated sugar |
| 1 | egg |
| 1 | egg yolk |
| ¹/₄ | cup heavy cream |
| 2 | tsp. pure almond extract |
| 1 | tsp. pure vanilla extract |
| 2¹/₂ | cups all-purpose flour |
| 1 | tsp. baking powder |
| ¹/₂ | tsp. kosher salt |
| 3 | oz. semisweet bar chocolate, finely chopped |
| | Sparkling white sugar *or* turbinado sugar |

**Pulse** strawberries in a food processor until finely chopped to yield 1 cup.

**Cream** butter and granulated sugar in a large bowl with a mixer on medium speed until light and fluffy, about 5 minutes.

**Add** egg to creamed mixture; beat on medium speed to blend, then add egg yolk and beat until incorporated. Beat in heavy cream, almond extract, and vanilla.

**Whisk** together flour, baking powder, and salt; beat into creamed mixture until combined.

**Add** pulsed strawberries to dough; beat just to incorporate. Stir chocolate into dough and chill at least 30 minutes.

**Preheat** oven to 350°. Line baking sheets with parchment paper.

**Drop** cookies with a #40 scoop (1¹/₂ Tbsp.) onto prepared baking sheets; sprinkle with sparkling sugar.

**Bake** cookies until edges are set, 15–17 minutes. Let cookies cool 5 minutes on baking sheets, then transfer to a rack to cool completely.

Per cookie: 123 cal; 7g total fat (4g sat); 26mg chol; 30mg sodium; 15g carb (1g fiber, 8g total sugars); 1g protein

89

# PASSIONATE FOR
# RED
# VELVET

## RED VELVET COOKIES

*These yummy cookies are just the right amount of crispy and chewy with all the character, fun, and flavor of classic red velvet cake.*

Makes about 3 dozen cookies
Total time: 22 minutes + baking

| | |
|---|---|
| 3 | cups all-purpose flour |
| 1/2 | cup unsweetened cocoa powder |
| 1 | tsp. baking soda |
| 1/2 | tsp. table salt |
| 2 | sticks unsalted butter (16 Tbsp.), softened |
| 2 | cups sugar |
| 2 | eggs |
| 1 | Tbsp. liquid red food color |
| 2 | tsp. distilled white vinegar |
| 12 | oz. white bar chocolate, chopped |

**Preheat** oven to 375°. Line baking sheets with parchment paper.
**Whisk** together flour, cocoa, baking soda, and salt in a bowl.
**Cream** butter and sugar in a separate bowl with a mixer on medium speed until fluffy, 5 minutes. Beat in eggs, food color, and vinegar. Mix flour mixture into creamed mixture just to combine. Stir in white chocolate, cover, and chill dough 30 minutes.
**Scoop** dough with a #30 scoop (about 2 Tbsp.) onto prepared baking sheets. Bake cookies until edges are set, 12–14 minutes. Let cookies cool on baking sheet, 5 minutes, then transfer to a rack.

Per cookie: 175 cal; 8g total fat (5g sat); 24mg chol; 78mg sodium; 25g carb (1g fiber, 11g total sugars); 2g protein

**READER FAVORITE**

Our readers love these cookies — they're easy to make and full of red velvet color and flavor.

## RED VELVET CUPCAKES

*With its crimson color and snow white icing, these mini cakes are as cute and tasty as can be.*

Makes about 2 dozen
Total time: about 2 hours

- 3½ cups all-purpose flour
- 3 Tbsp. unsweetened cocoa powder
- 1½ tsp. *each* baking soda, table salt, and instant espresso powder
- 2 cups sugar
- 3 eggs
- 2 cups vegetable oil
- ¼ cup liquid red food color
- 1½ tsp. pure vanilla extract
- 1½ cups buttermilk
- 1½ tsp. distilled white vinegar

**Preheat** oven to 350°. Line two 12-cup muffin pans with paper liners.

**Whisk** together flour, cocoa, baking soda, salt, and espresso powder in a bowl; set aside.

**Blend** sugar and eggs in a bowl with a hand mixer on medium speed until ribbons form, about 5 minutes. With mixer running, add oil in a steady stream until blended. Mix in food color and vanilla until incorporated.

**Mix** half the dry ingredients into creamed mixture, followed by buttermilk and vinegar, then remaining dry ingredients; blend just until incorporated. Fill liners to the top with batter; bake until a toothpick inserted in centers of cupcakes comes out clean, 20–25 minutes. Cool cupcakes in pan 20 minutes, transfer to a rack to cool completely; frost with icing.

Per frosted cupcake: 366 cal; 21g total fat (4g sat); 27mg chol; 260mg sodium; 46g carb (1g fiber, 29g total sugars); 5g protein

# RED VELVET

The origins of red velvet cake are debatable, but one thing's for sure — cocoa powder is a must. The trademark color typically comes from food coloring, but even beets can be used to tint baked goods that bright red color.

## CLASSIC WHITE ICING

Makes 8 cups
Total time: 20 minutes + chilling

- 2½ cups whole milk
- ¾ cup all-purpose flour
- 2½ cups sugar
- 5 sticks unsalted butter, softened (2½ cups)
- 1 tsp. pure vanilla extract
  Cocoa powder

**Whisk** milk and flour together in a saucepan. Cook over medium heat until thick and smooth, about 5 minutes, whisking often.

**Boil** 1 minute to eliminate the starchy taste of the flour, whisking constantly. Transfer to a bowl and cover with plastic wrap, pressing it on the surface to prevent a skin from forming; chill until cold.

**Cream** sugar and butter in a bowl with a mixer on high speed until light and fluffy, about 5 minutes. Add vanilla and chilled milk mixture, beating to the consistency of whipped cream, about 5 minutes. Spoon frosting into a piping bag fitted with a large straight tip and pipe spirals onto cupcakes.

**Dust** with cocoa.

STAFF FAVORITE

When Haley developed this cookie recipe, we all went crazy for it, and we're sure you will too!

## NUTELLA COOKIES

*For chewy centers and crisp edges, remove the cookies from the oven when the centers look underdone.*

Makes 2 dozen (3-inch) cookies
Total time: 1¼ hours + chilling

**WHISK:**

| | |
|---|---|
| 2 | cups all-purpose flour |
| ¼ | cup unsweetened cocoa powder |
| ½ | tsp. *each* baking soda and table salt |

**BEAT:**

| | |
|---|---|
| 1 | stick unsalted butter (8 Tbsp.), softened |
| 1½ | cups sugar |
| 2 | eggs |
| 1 | cup Nutella |
| 1 | tsp. pure vanilla extract |
| | Finely chopped hazelnuts |

**Whisk** together flour, cocoa powder, baking soda, and salt.

**Beat** butter and sugar with a stand mixer on medium speed, 5 minutes. Add eggs one at a time, beating to fully incorporate before adding the next. Add Nutella and vanilla; beat until combined. Add flour mixture; mix just until combined. Chill dough 4 hours or overnight.

**Preheat** oven to 350°. Line baking sheets with parchment paper.

**Scoop** dough with a #30 scoop (about 2 Tbsp.); roll in hazelnuts. Bake cookies, six at a time, until edges are set, about 15 minutes. Let cookies cool completely on baking sheets.

Per cookie: 191 cal; 9g total fat (4g sat); 26mg chol; 86mg sodium; 25g carb (1g fiber, 9g total sugars); 3g protein

## GOOD TO KNOW

Called "the original hazelnut spread," Nutella is a unique blend of roasted hazelnuts, sugar, skim milk, and a hint of cocoa. It's popular in Europe as a spread on toast (think peanut butter in the U.S.). Find Nutella in the grocery aisle near the peanut butter.

**23** Grilled Broccoli & Red Onion Hoagies

**24** Italian Joe on ciabatta bread

**25** Hawaiian Pork Sliders & Hawaiian Pico de Gallo

**26** French Dip au Jus

**27** Celery Slaw

**28** Chicken Pomodoro

**30** Korean Bulgogi Tacos

**31** Pork & Shiitake Mushroom Congee

**33** Tex-Mex Lasagna

**33** Avocado-Lettuce Salad

**35** Rosé Wine-Steamed Mussels

**35** Crouton Fries

**36** Sesame-Crusted Salmon with wasabi dipping sauce

**37** Spicy Beef Fried Rice

**39** Chicken Tamale Pie

**39** Pinto Bean Salad with lemon-garlic vinaigrette

**40** Cuisine Poke Bowl

**40** Shrimp & Creamy Grits with tomato cream sauce

**42** Tofu Stir-Fry with black pepper sauce

**43** Cuban Black Beans & Quinoa

**44** Chicken Enchiladas

**45** Muffuletta Dutch Baby

**46** Prosciutto-Wrapped Pork Medallions with fiorentina sauce

**47** Three-Herb Falafel with tahini sauce

**49** Classic Southern Fried Chicken

**50** Chunky Tomato Gravy

**51** Rice Pilaf with collards

**51** Southern Sweet Tea with lime & mint

**52** Pecan-Crusted Chicken Salad

**53** Fried Chicken Sandwiches & Rémoulade with pimentos

**55** Japanese Fried Chicken

**55** Vinegar Sushi Rice

**57** Beef Filets with poivre butter

**57** Warm Vegetable Salad

**58** Pressure Cooker Carnitas

**59** Vietnamese Noodle Salad with grilled marinated pork

**60** Smoked Salmon Pasta with capers & dill

**62** Roasted Butternut Squash & whole-wheat penne

**63** Mexican Carbonara

**64** Cacio e Pepe

**65** Orechiette alla Norcina

**66** Ramen Noodles & Meatballs

**67** ONE-POT RAGU WITH ITALIAN SAUSAGE

**69** Boursin Chicken Lasagna

**70** Crab Mac 'N Cheese

**71** Spinach & Three Cheese Stuffed Shells

**73** Bolognese Cavatelli with meatballs

**74** Chocolate Chip Cookies

**77** Chocolate Cake & Glossy Chocolate Icing

**78** French Apple-Custard Pie

**81** Nectarine Torte with hazelnuts & orange

**83** Chocolate Truffle Cheesecake

**85** Chocolate-Crusted Seven-Layer Bars

**87** Chocolate-Covered Strawberry Shortcakes

**88** Strawberry Shortcake Bars with fresh strawberry topping

**89** Strawberry-Chocoloate Shortcake Cookies

**90** Red Velvet Cookies

**91** Red Velvet Cupcakes with Classic White Icing

**93** Nutella Cookies

# LET'S TALK FOOD

Introducing **Must Love Food,** a podcast meant to inspire and educate people who love to cook, eat, and learn about food. The Cuisine at Home staff gives you the **Inside Scoop** on what we're currently working on in our Test Kitchens along with **Table Talk**, an open, grab-bag discussion about a variety of topics. We're also interviewing other professionals in the food industry in our **Spill the Beans** segment. In **Top Shelf**, you'll learn about different wines, spirits, and what we're sipping on now. Send us your questions and we'll answer them to the best of our knowledge in **Free Range**. And to spice things up a bit we play a food-related trivia game in a segment called **Cracked Up**. And lastly, **Let's Make A Meal** is where we open our refrigerator, or yours, and make a meal from what's inside. We invite you to have a seat at our table, so subscribe and listen wherever you download your podcasts.

Must L✱ve FOOD

Made in the USA
Monee, IL
08 December 2021

84313314R00059